The
French Quarter
Drinking Companion

Photograph by John d'Addario

The
French Quarter
Drinking Companion

By Allison Alsup, Elizabeth Pearce, & Richard Read

PELICAN PUBLISHING COMPANY
Gretna 2013

*The word "Pelican" and the depiction of a pelican are
trademarks of Pelican Publishing Company, Inc., and are
registered in the U.S. Patent and Trademark Office.*

ISBN: 9781455618156
E-book ISBN: 9781455618163

Printed in Korea

Published by Pelican Publishing Company, Inc.
1000 Burmaster Street, Gretna, Louisiana 70053

Contents

Acknowledgments

The Tipplers (Allison Alsup, Elizabeth Pearce, and Richard Read) would like to give thanks to the many, many workers who keep the drinks flowing in the French Quarter, who lend an ear and give advice, who make spectacular cocktails, and who generally create an atmosphere of conviviality unmatched anywhere on Planet Earth. Without them, there'd be no magic.

We would like to thank Gordon Warnock for his initial work and support in finding a home for our book, our agent Andrea Hurst, as well as Barbara Herman and Marty Padgett. We are grateful to Pelican Publishing Company and our editor, Nina Kooij, for taking on the project.

On a personal note, we would like to thank those who encouraged this project and often accompanied us on our rounds: John d'Addario, Gavin MacArthur, Lee Domingue, Carolyn Pearce, and Tina Boudreaux.

Introduction

Man, liquor sure goes fast in hot weather.
—Stanley Kowalski, *A Streetcar Named Desire*

Well, honey, a shot never does a Coke any harm!
—Blanche DuBois, *A Streetcar Named Desire*

Drinking in New Orleans comes with the territory, literally. Our city is surrounded by water. It practically floats. New Orleans and its inhabitants are defined by a liquid landscape. In a city shaped like a bowl, its base dipping below sea level, we are the truest definition of a watering hole.

Beyond topography, drinking is embedded in our DNA. New Orleans was founded by the French, who've never been shy about their fondness for wine and spirits. According to legend, they settled the French Quarter—or *Vieux Carré* (Old Square), as they called it—during Carnival, the annual festival of whooping it up.

The French were followed by more Europans, including Spanish, Irish, and Italian settlers. Jews, Latin Americans, and others piled in—the point being that the one thing New Orleans has never, ever been is Puritan. Understand that, and you begin to understand our relationship with booze.

Oh, and did we mention that it's also the unofficial home of the cocktail and the city that Prohibition forgot? We never stood a chance at sobriety.

New Orleans now boasts more bars per capita than anywhere in the U.S. And if you're looking for the city's highest concentration of nightclubs, neighborhood pubs, lounges, and other boozy places, you'll find it in the French Quarter. In fact, there are well more than 100 places to fill your cup here. We Tipplers counted to 180 and gave up. The sheer number of establishments means that there's room for everything from tony, highfalutin' nightspots to holes in the wall that can make the skeeziest Tijuana dive bar look glamorous by comparison. The Quarter doesn't discriminate against any kind of drinking.

For drinkers afraid of commitment, this is your Holy Land. Once you're in the Quarter, there's no need to get in the car and drive from neighborhood to neighborhood. In a space that totals less than a square mile, every bar in the Quarter is accessible by foot or rickshaw. And since there are no cover charges, you'll never have to feel too invested in one spot. So the evening might start with martinis by a piano and end with pancakes and a mimosa. This capricious meandering is the essence of the Quarter, and here's something you should remember before you *can't*: how the evening begins isn't necessarily how it will end.

A Few Words Regarding New Orleans' Drinking Culture

Drinking in New Orleans is a little different from other parts of America. For starters, our bars don't have to close. Many of the ones in this book serve booze 24 hours a day, 365 days a year. In fact, there's a story dating from August 2005, when Hurricane Katrina was threatening to wash out the city and Mayor Ray Nagin issued a mandatory evacuation. The legend goes that employees at one French Quarter bar realized for the first time that the front doors didn't have locks. Why would they have needed them?

While round-the-clock service is certainly convenient, it also means that a bar's clientele changes throughout the day and night. Your fellow drinkers at 2:00 P.M. are undoubtedly (well, hopefully) going to be very, very different from the ones you encounter at 2:00 A.M. Since most people prefer to do their serious drinking after dark, in this book we tend to talk about the evening and nighttime crowds. But depending on when and where you do your tippling, you may see some holdovers from the previous "shift."

Another difference: in New Orleans, we can take our drinks on the street. (Did you expect anything different from the land of drive-through daiquiri shops?) The only catch is that on the street, whatever you're imbibing must be encased in plastic. Any bartender or waiter can happily provide you with a go-cup, so when you're wanting to wander, leave the breakables behind. In fact, carrying glass is one of the few things that can ruffle the feathers of New Orleans' legendarily *laissez-faire* police force.

In fact, not only *can* you carry your cocktail wherever you roam, we encourage you to do so. More than visiting any single bar, strolling through the Quarter, sipping a drink, and chatting with friends provide the quintessential New Orleans experience. There's nothing like passing through Jackson Square at midnight while clutching a Pimm's cup in one hand and fanning yourself with the other.

The Making of the 100

Some cities are best understood by their churches, parks, and industries. We feel that *drinking* is one of the best ways to understand the French Quarter. Drinking is fundamental to the identity of New Orleans. In other places, drinking may be tucked away, with nips taken on the sly or reserved for special occasions only. However, in the French Quarter, drinking is a daily ritual.

This book's purpose is to evoke what it's like to drink in the Quarter. While the entries can be read individually for the purposes of gathering typical guidebook information, our hope is that you will read all of our reviews and, in doing so, in some way experience the panorama of our drinking culture. Our book is designed to be different from other guides. We've been purposefully anecdotal because that's the way we see drinking in the Quarter—as an important part of the story of New Orleans.

When we set out to make our list of the French Quarter's 100 notable bars, we had a couple of criteria. First, of course, the bar must be located in the French Quarter, that neighborhood that runs from the Mississippi River to Rampart Street and from Canal Street to Esplanade Avenue. Heck, this is why we wrote this book in the first place. There are plenty of guides to New Orleans, but few are dedicated exclusively to its oldest neighborhood. Fewer guides still, if any, focus solely on bars—not restaurants, not hotels, but bars. Considering that the Quarter is where most visitors spend their time and where many locals come to celebrate, that seems odd, doesn't it? We aim to fix that with this book.

We did make one exception for one very special bar, but the Sazerac is so legendary that its reputation swells across Canal Street.

Our second criterion was that the bar had staying power. Bars, like other businesses, are subject to the whims of consumers. The right location, ambiance, price point, and management can ensure years of success. Screw up one of those—or more—and a bar can go under in weeks.

For the most part, the watering holes in this book have been around for years, some for decades and quite a few for over a century. The new places on our list made the cut either because we have faith in their owners or because they're simply the latest iteration of a bar in the same location. For example, several hotel bars have changed names and even owners over the years, but somehow, the bars and their clientele have remained the same.

That doesn't mean that all of the places on our list are perfect. True, some are spectacular. Some rank as the best of their kind in the world. Others are more like anthropological experiments—

not the kind of place where we'd want to hang out every day but important to visit at least once. Not every bar on this list will appeal to every tippler. Nor are our reviews necessarily an endorsement of a bar for our favorites, which are listed at the back of the book. But that doesn't mean that you, dear reader, won't have the time of your life in any of the bars reviewed here.

Our reviews are based on our own visits and may vary greatly from others' experiences in the same bar. Though we've tried to capture the general feel of each bar, our stories are not necessarily representative of the ones you will tell. Our opinions shouldn't be taken as definitive judgments on the bars, only as snapshots of our experiences.

A final disclaimer: we were drinking while we wrote this thing. The details of our adventures were sometimes fuzzy the next morning. Other times, we've merged similar incidents into a single, representative review. And of course, we've left out the more boring parts. But it's generally a true account of our adventures.

Even if you never visit New Orleans (though we hope you do), please join us for a round as a guest Tippler. Before you turn the page, though, we invite you to pour yourself a drink.

CHAPTER 1

Iconic Bars

It's no secret: New Orleanians love to drink. Throughout the last 300 years or so, the city has been home to thousands of bars, juke joints, taverns, pubs, and lounges, most of which have disappeared without much ado. But a handful of bars have earned a very special place in the hearts and livers of drinkers—bars that have become mainstays of the French Quarter landscape. These markers have altered where we go, where we meet, even which sidewalks we congregate on.

Like the city itself, New Orleans iconic bars are a diverse lot. Some, like the glamorous Carousel Bar, are decidedly upscale. Others, like brick-and-beam Lafitte's Blacksmith Shop, are down to earth. What binds them together is that they're all characters. Distinct and unmistakable, these iconic establishments are here for the long haul. They're not gimmicky or trendy. They're just perfect places for drinking, for gossiping with friends and making new ones. If you visit no other bars in the Quarter, you'll do well to visit these.

Name: Carousel Bar

Address: 214 Royal Street (in the Monteleone)

Phone: 504-523-3341

Web site: www.HotelMonteleone.com

Your tab: You're at a hotel bar, and you're at the upper end of the Quarter, so it's not going to be cheap. At $15, the specialty martinis are some of the priciest menu items, as they are in other joints. But most run-of-the-mill cocktails are about half that price.

What you're swilling: The Carousel Bar isn't about compromise. If they don't have it in stock, it's probably not worth drinking. Feeling especially decadent? Have a negroni, a half-bitter, half-sweet aperitif. Or try a "Death in the Afternoon"—a cocktail invented by Ernest Hemingway that consists of a shot of absinthe topped off with champagne. It seems appropriate, since the Carousel Bar was one of Papa's favorite watering holes.

What you're wearing: There's no official dress code, but this place looks like a million bucks. At least have the courtesy to leave your flip-flops at home.

What you're hearing: The Monteleone added an area for live music performances. Check the Web site to see who's playing on any given night.

Tattoo themes: It's not uncommon to see ink peeking from underneath a shirtsleeve or partially obscured by the straps of a sundress. But for the crowd at the Carousel Bar, tattoos are incidental, not a centerpiece.

Your drinking buddies: A healthy mix of tourists and old-school New Orleanians, out for a night on the town. The crowd varies a bit, but it's safe to say that most in the room are over 30.

Best feature: Are you kidding? The namesake Carousel Bar in the center of the front room. Grab a seat if you can, and enjoy the view as it rotates. (Don't worry, it moves slowly, so no one's going to hurl—well, unless you're really, really hammered, in which case, might we recommend the banquette?)

The Carousel has changed since the last time we were here. That's a good thing. For years, the Carousel's giant bar was jammed into a room just off the lobby of the Hotel Monteleone. It still is, and it still dominates that room, but the wall on the far side has now been removed. Guests who can't find a seat at the bar or on one of the banquettes can slip through to a new, airy lounge area.

And that's exactly where we go. It's a Saturday afternoon, and the Carousel "proper" is packed to the gills. So we make our way to a couple of sofas in the back, which provide a great view of Royal Street.

On the upside, this new space comes with its own, more user-friendly bar. At the namesake Carousel Bar, wedging yourself between sitting guests to order a drink can be a little weird: unless you stand very close to the bar, it's going to spin right by you. The bartenders are pros, so it's no big deal for them, but for the rest of us, it's unsettling.

The downside is that the back bar comes equipped with a flat-screen TV, making it feel like a sports joint. Not that there's anything wrong with sports joints *per se*, but it's not the sort of thing we'd expect at one of New Orleans' most iconic watering holes.

But whatever: a couple of negronis later, we're not thinking of that. We're deep in conversation with a couple of tourists from New York, trading insights on the best-kept secrets in our respective hometowns. They rattle off restaurant after restaurant and bar after bar that we've never heard of, which makes us feel like slackers when they ask, "So, where's the best place to get a drink in New Orleans?"

After a short pause, Richard replies, "You're soaking in it."

Name: Lafitte's Blacksmith Shop
Address: 941 Bourbon Street
Phone: 504-593-9761
Web site: www.lafittesblacksmithshop.com
Your tab: Reasonable if you order beer and well drinks
What you're swilling: They feature a specialty purple drink, but it's awfully sweet. Stick with the standards.
What you're wearing: Anything goes here, from tourist shorts to formal apparel.
What you're hearing: Rowdy sing-along piano playing
When you're there: Most folks come here at night, but we love drinking on the sidewalk on a quiet afternoon.
Tattoo themes: Demure to daring
Your drinking buddies: Tourists checking it off the list and locals who still keep it on theirs
Best feature: The building itself

Lafitte's Blacksmith Shop contends it is the oldest operating bar in the United States, and there's little reason to doubt it. The building was erected between 1722 and 1732 near the house of local hero and privateer Jean Lafitte. Though there is no record of him actually drinking at this bar, proximity leads to probability, so in all likelihood, Jean Lafitte knocked back a few here long ago.

The records of early New Orleans government are peppered with attempts to control liquor sales, to little avail. When French governor Vaudreuil set limits on the number of taverns and their hours, he was blithely ignored. In 1763, after the new Spanish governor announced a cap of 13 taverns in the city, his office was immediately plagued with petitions to increase it to 38. So it seems fitting that at least one of those early establishments has continued to serve the city since that time. While we've been governed under 10 flags, our drinking has remained a constant.

At our table near a window, we sip our $5 beers and hear the story of Jean Lafitte, courtesy of the buggy driver who has parked his rig in our view. He regales his riders with tales of dubious veracity, but our growing buzz makes us tolerant of his mixture of fable, lore, and outright falsehood. His inaccuracies, we begrudgingly admit, are an integral part of the French Quarter's magic, a place where distinguishing between truth and fiction has never been a high priority.

The clip-clop of the mule fades down Bourbon Street, and that 18th-century sound mingles perfectly with the historic brick-and-post construction that surrounds us. The bar's only illumination is candlelight, and now that dusk has turned to dark, patrons are compelled to lean in to see each other. This motion repeats at each table, and the bar fills with a tableau of spies and illicit lovers plotting intrigue.

We prefer Lafitte's on weeknights, when the room offers the promise of a clandestine tryst or furtive observation. On weekend nights, the cloak-and-dagger whispers are challenged by the cacophony of the piano bar, where well-oiled patrons lustily belt out "Me and Bobby McGee." If you wish to escape the commotion, amble out to the tiny patio, where even on a sweltering summer evening you can catch a cool river breeze. But tonight we remain inside the quiet bar, listening to the murmur of patrons making plans, perhaps noble, perhaps unlawful, perhaps mundane, but all made in the grand tradition of New Orleans: with a drink.

Photograph by John d'Addario

Name: Napoleon House
Address: 500 Chartres Street (at St. Louis Street)
Phone: 504-524-9752
Web site: www.NapoleonHouse.com
Your tab: Average. Tack on some reasonably priced food to help absorb the booze.
What you're swilling: Napoleon House is an institution, and one look at the bar will tell you why. If these guys can't make it, you shouldn't be drinking it. However, their Pimm's cup is legendary.
What you're wearing: There's no dress code to speak of, but Napoleon House is one of the most picturesque bars in the city, if not the world. Don't ruin the ambiance for your fellow tipplers by showing up in grubby cutoffs and a tank top.
What you're hearing: Opera and classical music, nonstop
Tattoo themes: Everyone has a little ink nowadays, but here, it tends to be well covered up.
Your drinking buddies: A goodly number of tourists, but you're prone to hear a few local accents bouncing off the stuccoed walls, too. The crowd doesn't hail from the shuffleboard set, but they're not super young, either. Just behave yourself.

Best feature: Generally speaking, it's a tossup between the front bar (which probably hasn't been redecorated since the Battle of New Orleans) and the charming courtyard. If you're here for a special event, though, you might just get to see the stunning "Appartement de l'Empereur" on the second floor. Rumors abound of secret rooms built to hide Napoleon after his planned escape from Elba. Alas, they're only rumors, so far as we know—or at least they're not on view.

Entering the Napoleon House can be unsettling. Or maybe "unsettling" is the wrong word. "Striking" might be better.

The Napoleon House sits at the bustling corner of St. Louis and Chartres streets, opposite the swanky, shiny Omni Royal Orleans hotel and diagonally across from the refurbished Supreme Court building. Combined, those two Beaux Arts facades are pretty imposing. But swing open the narrow door to the Napoleon House, and you step into a much older world: one that's dimly lit, with amber slants of sunlight splayed across well-worn wooden tabletops that have seen their share of spilled booze and cigarette burns over the years. Opera plays at a respectable but not ear-shattering level. The walls have a patina that Hollywood set designers would have a hard time matching—because it's real.

Unlike the buildings across the street, the Napoleon House was built on a human scale. The ceiling seems low, even though it's not, and the place doesn't feel as if it's changed much in 200 years.

The story goes that Napoleon House is so named because it was here, in this bar, that notorious pirate Jean Lafitte and his pals hatched a plan to rescue Napoleon from his prison on Elba Island and move him to New Orleans. (Of course, that raises the question of what Napoleon House was called before it became the Napoleon House, but whatever: details can ruin a good story.)

Today, about the only signs of Napoleon you'll find at the Napoleon House are a bust of the itty-bitty emperor behind the bar and a poster on the wall. The other faces in the place represent a good mix of tourists and locals (though mostly tourists) enjoying well-made drinks, served by a wait staff of men in white shirts and bowties.

If you're only here for the drinking, you'll probably be seated in the front room—either at the bar or at one of a dozen or so tables. If you're hungry, they're more likely to seat you in the spectacular (though intimate) courtyard or the slightly more formal dining room. And if you happen to stumble in for a party . . . well, you're in luck, because the "Appartement de l'Empereur" on the second floor is a little slice of magic.

As we settle into our favorite table—the one in the middle of the room with an inlaid chessboard (no playing pieces, sadly)—we turn to the waiter and unanimously say, "Pimm's cup, please." This isn't much of a shocker. No one in town comes close to the Napoleon House in making these quintessentially British cocktails, which are light and smooth as lemonade but with a much bigger kick.

We pass the time gossiping about the latest New Orleans news, stopping now and then to eavesdrop on a couple of nearby tables. One group is chatting about Hové, a local *parfumerie* half a block away that one of them had stumbled into. (FYI, their vetiver bath gel is amazing.) Another foursome is contemplating a midafternoon snack. Richard can't help himself and turns to face them.

"Split a muffaletta. It's one of the best in town."

They thank him for his suggestion—warily. It's obvious that they're not used to interacting with strangers so casually, but a few drinks down the road, they've changed their tune.

An hour later—after the foursome has inhaled their muffaletta and peppered us with questions about other local restaurants—we stumble out into the late afternoon sun, a little shocked to return to a world filled with automobiles and smartphones.

Name: Pat O'Brien's
Address: 718 St. Peter Street
Phone: 504-525-4823
Web site: www.patobriens.com
Your tab: Midrange, depending on how much you tip the piano players to play "Sweet Caroline"
What you're swilling: Hurricanes by the gallon, though Budweiser and Abita show up a lot, too
What you're wearing: Your bridesmaid dress, your football team's jersey, matching bachelorette-party T-shirts, khakis and your frat's logo
What you're hearing: Lots of visiting in the patio, but the piano bar is all lounge standards
When you're there: Before the game, after the wedding, Christmas Eve, day and night
Tattoo themes: Not too many visible
Your drinking buddies: Fellow wedding-party members, your high-school or college mates, your family
Best feature: The Fountain of Fire

For locals, Pat O'Brien's is inevitable. Whether making a stop on your 21st birthday, accompanying out-of-town visitors, or deciding on a lark to "play tourist," sooner or later, whether you want to or not, you're seated in the piano bar, roaring along with the other hundred bodies to "Margaritaville," never sure if you are doing so ironically. But if you're here once again, sipping on a hurricane you didn't intend to order, you might as well enjoy it. Pat O'Brien's slogan is "Have Fun!" and by the end of the night, even we jaded local Tipplers had succumbed to the bar's charms.

The courtyard's ample drinking space permits groups to cobble chairs and tables together and create the seating needed for parties of 10, 20, or more. The sheer number of people drinking around us differentiates Pat O's (as locals affectionately call it) from most patio bars. It is not intimate. Instead, the night starts

Photograph by John d'Addario

lively and ends up rowdy, a rollicking sea of bobbing hurricane glasses illuminated by the red, orange, and yellow flames that dance in the spray of the courtyard's huge center fountain.

Post-reception wedding parties arrive, tuxedos askew and bowties abandoned, the bridesmaids having eschewed pumps for flip-flops. Herds of bachelorettes crowd the area, sporting banners announcing their upcoming nuptials. Legions of sports fans stake out turf and tonight are particularly vocal before an upcoming championship game, engaging in dueling fight songs, like in *Casablanca* but without the Nazis. And of course, no one is trying to leave.

We choose gin and tonics over hurricanes, and you should, too. As much as you may want to sample this drink at its source, be warned: they are pretty terrible here. The original recipe made with passion-fruit juice creates a delicious drink. Today, volume demands that Pat O's sacrifice quality for quantity, so the cocktail's current incarnation starts with a Kool-Aid base and tastes of chemical and disappointment. Still, it is a pleasure to watch waiters bearing trays of the gaudy lantern-shaped glasses to other tables. Those on a budget, take note: you can exchange your glass for cash. We know savvy locals who scour empty tables for abandoned hurricane glasses and turn them in for drinking money. It's a thrifty trick.

After finishing our first drink there, we are ready for a different venue. But before moving to the piano bar, Allison and Elizabeth head to the loo. NB: if ya gotta go, the upstairs ladies' restroom is one of the nicest in the French Quarter. Take a cushy seat and chat with your girlfriends as you apply lipstick. Refresh yourself with perfume from a restroom attendant who offers amenities and towels. After hitting johns of dubious quality, you will appreciate the oasis that is the Pat O'Brien's ladies room.

We all meet again in the piano lounge, where the dueling pianos thunder away. The musicians are as deft at crowd management as they are at pounding out the standards. We join in on "House of the Rising Sun," promising to "tell our children not to do as we have done." Everything you expect to hear is here: "Piano Man," "New York, New York," and "Sweet Caroline." Though the piano players seem to be having a good time, we wonder how they stand playing the LSU fight song night after night. We salute birthdays ranging from 21 to 80 and anniversaries from the 1st to the 40th. We also hear people doing their part to continue a family tradition, drinking in the same bar as their parents and grandparents.

This joint singing merges us with the larger crowd: an odd sensation to have in a bar. Collective energy is more common while singing in church or shouting at a football game with likeminded people, not with a group of folks you haven't even met. Unlike other bars, where you might merely feel welcome, Pat O'Brien's provides you with a group to join. Some may call that a refuge; others may call it a cult. If you start thinking about it too much, it's disconcerting. But the drinks are there to keep us from thinking. We close our eyes and join in for another round of "Sweet Caroline," singing and swaying as one.

Name: Sazerac Bar
Address: 123 Baronne Street (in the Roosevelt Hotel)
Phone: 504-648-1200
Web site: www.theroosevelt.com (a Web site worth reading, for its snapshots of the bar's history and former governor Huey P. Long's connection to the hotel)
Your tab: $12 per drink, including tip
What you're swilling: Do you have to ask?
What you're wearing: A tie, a bridesmaid dress, something natty
What you're hearing: Classic jazz, but more likely the crowd
When you're there: Daily 11:00 A.M.–2:00 A.M. (the Sazerac is one of the few bars respectable enough to have hours)
Tattoo themes: Hidden
Your drinking buddies: Tasteful friends, dates, business colleagues, wealthy relations
Best feature: Service

We've gathered on Elizabeth's birthday, surrounded by friends. It's not unusual to be in the Sazerac on someone's birthday, for it's the kind of bar that invites punctuating life's accomplishments: engagements, graduations, anniversaries, a good haircut.

With its windowless, wooden-paneled walls and coved ceilings, the Sazerac evokes a faintly nautical feel. As we step up to the long curve of the immaculately polished bar, it's not much of a stretch to imagine we've stepped back in time and aboard the *Mauritania* or the *Lusitania* or any of the ocean-liners (post-*Titanic,* thank you) that once steered wealthy Americans across the Atlantic en route to their grand European tours. Indeed, the Sazerac is symbolically linked to river and ocean. Its architecture reminds visitors what's easy to lose sight of in the maze of the Quarter, namely that New Orleans is a port city and home to the longest wharf in the world. The original 1930s murals by American Paul Ninas lining the walls attest to the city's connection to the waterfront. (Note: they also attest to the fact that African-Americans were the ones loading and unloading the docks.)

As one of our friends, a former architecture professor who just happens to be still articulate enough to describe such matters, says, it's not surprising that the bar feels like a ship and different from the Victorian and antebellum proportions that rule the Quarter. Art Deco was an expression of our nation's newfound faith in industry, technology, and transportation. (Disclosure: Tippler conversations aren't usually this clever.) He notes that the period marked the first time we wanted our buildings to look *forward* to the future rather than back at the past. Ironically, such an implicit belief in the future of steam engines and automobiles almost seems nostalgic now. However, what can't be denied is that an upbeat optimism still reigns over the Sazerac.

But before we sail any further, let's concede a point to the landlubbers: the Sazerac Bar is not in the French Quarter. In coming here, the Tipplers have crossed over the breakers of the Vieux Carré and cruised a half-block past Canal. Yet we would be remiss in not including the Sazerac Bar in our 100, for it's the exception that proves the rule.

The history of New Orleans drinking doesn't begin with the Sazerac (no doubt that began before even making land), but the Big Easy's link to cocktails do. First concocted in the mid-19th century by the pharmacist Antoine Peychaud, of Peychaud's bitters, the Sazerac "coque-tail" supposedly offered medicinal benefits and, no doubt, profit. As far as the Tipplers are concerned, the intervening years have done nothing to diminish the drink's health benefits, and the Sazerac remains the official, unofficial cocktail of the Crescent City.

Buyers beware: at $10 for its namesake drink, the Sazerac is a sipping bar by New Orleans standards. But settle into one of the plush chairs or sofas, and you will probably concede that $10 is a small price to pay for a finely crafted Sazerac swirled with Herbsaint that numbs the lip and the pain of the world.

Nor is a 10-spot so much considering the attentive, experienced waitperson who now glides across the floor bearing not only our cocktails but also carafes of ice water and polished round trays containing wasabi peas, Chex mix, and a Tippler's favorite, local Zapp's Spicy Crawtator chips.

Suddenly, we feel cared for, tended to, and indeed *hopeful,* like first-class travelers looking forward to adventures. In the glow of the soft lights and table lamps, everyone appears slightly more attractive, their shoes decidedly more expensive against the carpet. Indeed, everyone appears like a contender to become the heir of a fabulous estate. Outside may be a world of ripped vinyl seats, plastic cups, and linoleum floors that must be hosed down before dawn. But here, at least for a little while, we can float and feel the weight of the world lift as the crisp-shirted server returns to refill our *water* glasses and someone comments about "relying on the kindness of strangers." Luddites, aesthetes, closet and freely admitted snobs, welcome to your refuge, at least for one round.

Photograph by John d'Addario

Name: Tujague's
Address: 823 Decatur Street (at Madison Street)
Phone: 504-525-8676
Web site: www.TujaguesRestaurant.com
Your tab: Average to just above average. You won't find "big-ass beers" here, but you will find perfectly made cocktails. Here, as elsewhere, you get what you pay for.
What you're swilling: Take your pick—there's a full assortment of booze behind the bar. If it's late and you're heading home, try a Sazerac. They've been making 'em here for a century and a half. Their swinging old fashioned features a secret mix of bitters.
What you're wearing: Folks in the dining room tend to dress up a bit, perhaps out of respect for the classic Creole menu. In the saloon, the attitude is more casual, but flip-flops may still feel out of place.
What you're hearing: If you're lucky, just the tinkle of cocktail glasses, the clop-clop-clop of mule-buggies, and the strains of a brass band playing for the folks at Café Du Monde across the street
Tattoo themes: Hard to say: most are covered up.
Your drinking buddies: Friendly types. They may not all be well heeled, but they're almost always well behaved. In the restaurant, the crowd is often about half New Orleanians and half tourists. In our experience, however, the saloon can skew much more local.
Best feature: The bar itself. From the stunning antique mirror to the old-school brass foot rail, they just don't make 'em like that anymore.

If you're not looking for Tujague's, it's easy to miss. Sure, there's a large neon sign stretching up the side of the building, boasting the year the place opened: 1856. But even so, Tujague's has a hard time standing out from the garish T-shirt shops and other tourist magnets littering its territory on Decatur Street.

To the casual visitor, Tujague's can look equally unassuming on the inside. It feels like the sort of place your grandfather would have frequented when he was your age—and he very well might have. Like a gracefully aging grande dame, Tujague's wears its years proudly. It doesn't try to seduce you with sleek, asymmetrical flower arrangements or trendy, recessed lighting. Tujague's relies on character—pure 19th-century character.

It's a sweltering summer afternoon as the three of us walk up Decatur, en route from the French Market to catch a movie at Canal Place. The thought of sitting in a dark, air-conditioned theater, munching on a giant tub of popcorn, seems decadent and perfect today. But as is often the case in New Orleans, Mother Nature has plans of her own. In the time it takes us to traverse two city blocks, clouds bubble up out of the blue, turning the sky a dark, angry gray-black. Sixty seconds later, it's pouring. We dash for the nearest open door: Tujague's.

Our eyes adjust to the gloom, and we find that we're the only people in the place. We step up to the bar and perch our soaked shoes on its renowned brass foot rail. A few minutes ago, we would have given our eyeteeth for a refreshing beer, but now, we're wet and chilly: whiskey all around, please.

Thunderstorms often bring life to a halt here. It's not unusual to see people huddled under balconies, chatting with strangers and waiting for the weather to let up. It may seem like an inconvenience, but in fact, it's a welcome pause, as refreshing as the rain pouring down from the sky.

Today's rain doesn't last long—in summer, it rarely does. By the time we hit the bottom of our drinks, it's not even drizzling, and we're free to keep strolling up steamy Decatur Street, fortified.

CHAPTER 2

The Bourbon Street Experience

Welcome to America's most debauched boulevard. Bourbon Street doesn't generate fair-to-middling responses. You either love it for its boisterous enthusiasm, or you hate it for . . . well, its boisterous enthusiasm. It's loud, obnoxious, and soaked through with beer, mystery punch, jello shots, grenades, daiquiris, and an ever-fermenting ale of human scent. The nine blocks stretching from Canal to Dumaine are the most intense, what cultural anthropologists call a "ludic zone," a place where folks from more restrained corners of the globe can blow off a little steam. For better or worse, the seven-nights-a-week, 24-hours-a-day, drink-till-you-drop (and we have seen it) Bourbon Street is what comes to mind when most visitors think of New Orleans.

To the untrained eye, Bourbon Street seems full of nothing but tourists and neon—and it's true, there are a lot of both. But look closer and you'll find hidden gems, places packed with locals, where good cocktails and great conversation are the order.

Photograph by John d'Addario

Name: Cat's Meow
Address: 701 Bourbon Street
Phone: 504-523-2788
Web site: www.catskaraoke.com
Your tab: Not bad if you only need three, as in three for one
What you're swilling: Booze and a mixer, beer
What you're wearing: Spandex, T-shirts, Ed Hardy
What you're hearing: Your fellow patrons singing or doing something like singing
When you're there: The lighting onstage looks better at night and so will you.
Tattoo themes: From military to hipster to punk. Karaoke knows no boundaries.
Your drinking buddies: Some come to sing. Some are dragged. None can look away.
Best feature: The karaoke, natch

Most entertainment in the United States is passive: we go to movies, concerts, and sporting events . . . and we watch, experiencing moments but rarely creating them. But visitors in the French Quarter soon realize that they are as much a part of the city's audacity, vulgarity, and beauty as the mimes, the musicians, the buggy drivers, and the strippers. Drinkers in the Quarter are an integral part of its spectacle but especially so at the Cat's Meow, where they *are* the show.

Cat's Meow performers croon on a real stage warmed by some sweet lighting. Small tables hug the edge of the stage, just like in Vegas, setting the scene for patrons to live out their musical dreams. Two pianos, painted hot pink and green and accented with leopard and zebra prints respectively, are moored on the back of the stage, though we don't know why. The only music is played with the click of a button.

It's an early Thursday evening and a handful of patrons sip on drinks, scanning the list of possible songs and weighing the merits of "Don't Stop Believin'" versus "We Got the Beat."

Our emcee, Abby, part cheerleader, part cruise director, keeps the action moving. She announces the next singer, Tiffany, who tosses back her cosmopolitan and takes the stage. Tiffany channels Celine Dion via her multimillion-dollar set up at Caesar's Palace and treats us to an unforgettable rendition of *Titanic*'s theme, because no matter how hard we try, we cannot forget it. While our hearts go on and on, we hit the bar and are rewarded with three-for-one robust whiskey and sodas.

A white board next to the stage alerts us that Randy is up next. "Sweet Child of Mine" starts, but the lyrics elude him, despite their scrolling presence on the monitors in front of the stage. Abby sings along a bit and finally turns to the audience, encouraging us to help him out. "Where do we goooo? Awww, awww, where do we go now?!"

The white board brims with names eager for their three and a half minutes of fame. Abby sings well and entertains us in the intervals between performances, luring patrons onto the stage/dance floor. We wonder if this is the kind of job she dreamed of when she was singing show tunes in her high-school choir. She grooves to Usher, and soon everyone is "getting low."

Upstairs at "The Cat" is a second, smaller bar overlooking the first floor, where we have an aerial view of Stacy's Bachelorette Party singing en masse. Below the second-floor balcony, Bourbon Street is quieter than the karaoke inside. We finish our drinks in this oddly located moment of peace and then head to our next bar, "Summer Lovin'" following us out the door.

Daiquiri Shops

Fellow Tipplers:

This isn't a standard bar entry, but we include it as part of our 100 because frozen daiquiris are an essential part of drinking in Louisiana. Frozen-daiquiri shops are so abundant in the French Quarter, especially along Bourbon Street, that we felt you deserved a broader context for their existence and the unique relationship our city has with the frozen concoction.

It can be difficult for some, especially those from the healthy or snowy states, to believe that drive-through daiquiri shops are legal in Louisiana. They're a bit like Sasquatch, since all the photos taken by witnesses are likely to be blurry. While our laws do go so far as to prohibit the actual consumption of alcohol while driving, la Louisiane is home to above-board, drive-through daiquiri shops—hundreds of them, perhaps thousands.

But don't just take the Tipplers' word. Drive-through daiquiri shops have been proven to exist. Indeed both the *Oregonian's Politifact* and "Inside Edition" have seen the need to prove the reality of drive-through daiquiri shops to otherwise disbelieving readers and viewers. And at least one Tippler can verify that one can legally drink and *ride,* after witnessing a couple dismount from their horses near the levee, tether the reins, and get a pair of daiquiris for the long ride back to the stable.

Of course, safety measures are in place to ensure that drivers don't drink while on the road. Every daiquiri shop must place a piece of tape over the straw hole, hand over the straw separately, and tell drivers something like, "Now you know you have to wait till you get home to drink that."

Not every Louisianian thinks daiquiri drive-throughs are a good idea. There even may be as many as three. One of them is State Sen. Dan Claitor, of Baton Rouge, who introduced the highly controversial Senate Bill 134 in February 2012. Though written in broad language, it was designed to target Louisiana's ubiquitous daiquiri drive-through industry. Claitor claimed that the perforated lids of go-cups from businesses such as Daiquiri Island, Daiquiri Planet, Daiquiri Hut, Daiquiri Paradise, Daiquiris and Company, Daiquiris and Creams, Bayou Daiquiri, New Orleans Original Daiquiris, Daiquiri Express, and Daiquiris to Go violate the state's open-container law.

However, Claitor, a former assistant district attorney for New Orleans, wanted it to be known that he wasn't aiming to shut down daiquiri drive-throughs but only that he drew the line at the straw perforations in the lids. Apparently, the holes *needed to go*. Claitor theorized that without straw slits, drivers would keep their drinks in their cup holders, unconsumed. Of course, everyone was shocked to learn that apparently those little pieces of tape have not been preventing drivers from sipping at their 64 ounces of frozen goodness of rum, tequila, vodka, and red food coloring while on the road.

"I don't see why anyone would oppose this," Claitor said of the bill.

Oh, Dan.

To most Louisianans, the senator's comment seems quaint by now. Not only was the public vocally against Claitor's bill, calling it a waste of time and pointless, they opposed the same bill two years before, when it was shot down in committee and never reached the floor. As Tipplers know, every few years we'll hear about these attempts on the radio, each earning about six seconds of coverage by WWOZ. To what degree Louisiana's frozen-daiquiri lobby (and you can bet there is one) plays a part in ending the debate, we'll never know.

And while the Tipplers do want to know more, lucid commentary can be challenging to find. In one of the more coherent editorials on Claitor's bill, *The Hayride,* an established blog of conservative commentary on Louisiana politics, questioned whether "daiquiri places ought to be regulated at all" and called SB 134 a "restriction on individual freedom." Give me libation or give me death. But the Tipplers prefer the deft wording of this opposed citizen who tried to offer some cultural context to other Americans reading the story: "Louisiana isn't like the rest of the union."

So while the Tipplers would like to present some facts and stats about Louisiana's frozen-daiquiri business, we're not sure they exist. The Tipplers have tried to determine just how many daiquiri shops, drive-through or otherwise, operate statewide. We've attempted to discover their net annual revenue. Perhaps the numbers are being kept secret. Or perhaps they're incalculable. It's also possible that no one in Louisiana has ever counted that high.

Tippler Frozen Daiquiri Facts

1. Drive-through daiquiri shops rate number 12 on the popular WordPress site *Stuff Cajun People Like,* just after number 11—feeling superior to Mississippi.

2. There are currently 17 bars along the seven-block stretch of Bourbon between Iberville and St. Ann serving frozen daiquiris. If you throw in frozen grenade drinks, you can add in seven more. For the record, this information was earned the hard way.

3. Addresses, hours, clothing, and tattoo themes are irrelevant when it comes to daiquiri shops in the Quarter. In fact, most things become irrelevant within their Day-Glo walls. They are not destinations. Three chains—Mango Mango, Big Easy Daiquiri, and Jester Daiquiri—dominate the Bourbon Street trade. The Tipplers have no evidence to suggest that one neon establishment is better than another. A few independent bars also have machines behind the bar.

4. Daiquiri prices are almost regulated in the Quarter: as of this writing, a 20-ounce daiquiri costs $9; an even bigger one costs $12. You may qualify for a free shooter, but you have to down it in the shop and hand the glass test tube back.

5. Peach Bellini tastes slightly better than apple Bellini.

6. Despite their bright colors and the fact that you can sample (like ice cream) before you buy, daiquiris are not for children. Daiquiris can contain multiple alcohols such as rum, vodka, and tequila, in proofs as high as 190.

7. Do not expect a paper umbrella.

8. Straw slit or no straw slit, no one, including Senator Claitor, needs to worry about drinking and driving when getting a frozen daiquiri in the Quarter. No one voluntarily drives down Bourbon, and if you at one point arrived by car, by the time you've finished your daiquiri, it is very likely you will have forgotten where you parked.

Name: Famous Door
Address: 339 Bourbon Street (at Conti Street)
Phone: 504-598-4334
Your tab: Seven dollars per drink
What you're swilling: Kamikaze shooters in Day-Glo colors, Budweiser, full bar available
What you're wearing: Boas and beads
What you're hearing: '80s cover bands
When you're there: After 10:00 P.M.
Tattoo themes: Too dark to see
Your drinking buddies: Tourists
Best feature: Tourists

It's the Saturday before Halloween. It's unusually brisk this year, a real autumn, and after 10:00 P.M., Bourbon Street begins to swell. Night after night, partying appears to be an inexhaustible human resource on Bourbon, but this evening the crowd is especially fueled by the naughtier associations of the holiday. As the Tipplers weave through the costumed crowd, heavy on Jack Sparrow and all things pirate, we pass the inevitable small pack of Christians holding Bibles as they circle round a cross and attempt to preach to a pair of sassy Trojan soldiers. A block later, we spot two "nuns" hopping up the steps into Temptations Gentlemen's Club.

The Famous Door (since 1934) isn't as large as some of the other clubs on Bourbon, and as a result, it easily feels packed. As we step inside, the emcee, a robust Catwoman, leads the audience through a line dance to "Footloose" and then gets the customers going for the returning band. As the group takes the stage, a Superhero theme emerges. We note the Captain America wastebasket propped up against the bass drum. Flash stands ready at the keyboards, while the gray-haired guitarist manages to exude a too-cool-for-Halloween vibe, capping his effort at an ancient Superman T-shirt and red wristbands. Batman, the backup vocalist, smokes through his mask.

The band launches into "Don't Stop Believin'" and tries to

make the Bourbon standard fresh *just one more time*. The crowd doesn't care. Arms pumping, people from all over the country turn to one another and overly mouth the words "living just to find emotion," as if deeply, deeply touched by the spirit of Steve Perry. Suddenly the Dark Knight jumps off the stage and returns with a round of Jäger. Downing his shot, he yells into the microphone, "Can somebody give me a f%&★ing scream?"

It can be hard to resist the collective thoughtlessness of Bourbon, so the Tipplers indulge in a round of blue shooters that smack of Otter Pops. We watch a female Ghostbusters team, complete with Slime and Stay-Puft, make their way towards the stage. But perhaps our favorite of the evening is the young couple who, judging by their North Face fleece jackets, hiking boots, pale complexions, and earnest, product-free hair, probably hail from Oregon. Moving front and center and with grins that say, "We're not allowed to do this in Eugene," they proceed to bump and squat in a most unwholesome way.

Trick or treat. In New Orleans, you get both.

Name: Funky 544
Address: 544 Bourbon Street
Phone: 504-599-9898
Your tab: Six to nine dollars per drink
What you're swilling: Three Abitas or three whiskeys. Three for one, so choose well. (Sorry, no three-for-one tooters, the lurid, neon-colored shots.)
What you're wearing: *Nothing excessively baggy,* according to the posted dress code
What you're hearing: Hip-hop
When you're there: After 9:00 P.M.
Tattoo themes: Names—people, frats, colleges
Your drinking buddies: Everyone and anyone. Our night includes locals, Southerners, Belgians, Brits, a Jamaican graciously giving away his third Jameson, and West Oakland.
Best feature: Balcony overlooking Bourbon

It's the prime Bourbon Street hour—Friday night, 10:00. A board on the doors explains the dress code: *no excessively baggy clothing.* Elizabeth looks down at her loose-fitting dress and says she may need to go home and change.

The Funky 544 has a split personality. Downstairs is a dark dance floor, heavy on hip-hop. Shot girls in low/high-cut black Lycra weave through the swaying crowd. The girls at 544 are known for being forward to the point of aggressiveness. They pop the closed ends of bright-red phallic test tubes in their mouths and jiggle as they point the open ends towards you. "No" isn't in their vocabulary. "No" simply means it's time for them to jiggle everything up and down.

On the stage is a young man with a microphone working the crowd. He isn't Hollywood handsome or cut, more like cute in a next-door sort of way: T-shirt, cap, jeans, and sneaks. Every now and again he claps his hands and echoes a line from whatever's playing. At first, we don't understand his role. He isn't a singer (though the 544 does feature live music as well) or even a dancer, and he isn't lip synching. We realize he's there to keep the mood upbeat, to model partying 544 style, and perhaps to cut off any tension that might erupt from the alcohol-fueled crowd. But from where the Tipplers are standing, the most aggressive behavior on the floor is from the shot girls.

"Are we ready to go home yet?" he calls out.

"No!" the crowd yells back.

"Give me a '*hell* no!'"

"Hell no!"

He points to a group near the stage. "West Oakland in the house! Remember, y'all, we got tooter shots for three dollars!"

How can we forget?

Up the narrow stairs lined with photos of R&B greats, the 544 feels distinctly different—smaller, brighter, with retro-issue damask wallpaper that evokes a bordello. The space centers around the bar and wall-mounted TVs showing football. It's quiet enough to talk. Signs promote "three for one everything." As a result, we end up with whiskey and sodas the size of a Big Gulp. The shooter girls pass through but aren't making the hard sells like on the dance floor below. However, the 544's principal attraction upstairs is located just outside the French doors—a balcony overlooking Bourbon.

While the balcony itself is simple and unexceptional, it's hard to underestimate the primal appeal of balconies on Bourbon for the heterosexual male. Of course, there's the implicit, apocryphal promise of flashing breasts and the chance to catcall with impunity. Balconies offer vantage points for watching girls and any action that passes below. But there's also the sense of prime *dominion,* of literally being above the fray.

As Gavin, one of our guest Tipplers, sips his never-ending three-for-one whiskey and soda, he notes that the sounds drifting in from the street remind him of bird mating rituals. With anthropological accuracy, he recites them: first, a deep cawing, followed by a higher-pitched "haw" in the distance. The deep caw is repeated, he explains, and again returned by the female. But on the third round, there is a change. The single low caw is joined by another male voice. The competition has begun.

Name: Johnny White's #2 Hole in the Wall
Address: 718 Bourbon Street
Phone: Doubtful
Web site: Fairly useless; Google it if you must
Your tab: Two to five dollars per drink
What you're swilling: Miller High Life, NOLA Golden Ale on draft, Maker's Mark
What you're wearing: Shorts, khakis, a Saints jersey
What you're hearing: Hole, XTC, Suzanne Vega, or the classic-rock-studded jukebox
When you're there: Nightly after 7:00, Sundays for games
Tattoo themes: Skulls and roses
Your drinking buddies: Locals, regulars, Saints fans, Redskins fans, and, like any Bourbon Street bar, tourists
Best feature: Tie between cheap drinks and man-cave ambiance

True to its Hole in the Wall nickname, JW #2 is slightly less sporty and even more of a dive than the original on St. Peter. It's the kind of place that looks full with 10 customers, and its decor can best be described as "rec room." For some guys, the #2 may represent the ultimate man cave—brownish walls, five televisions, sports and alcohol posters, a jukebox, video poker machines, and a seasonally decorated mounted moose head, all crammed into a single room.

But judging from the mantel underneath the moose and the French doors leading out to what might have once been a quaint courtyard, our guess is that a century ago, Johnny White's #2 was someone's front parlor and porch. So despite its location in the groin of Bourbon Street, the Hole in the Wall manages to feel apart from the mayhem, almost homey, and offers its customers a peek of the passing crowds from the comfort of padded stools.

Both Johnny White's call themselves sports bars, and perhaps because of this designation, they tend to be male heavy and attract customers who don't care about using outhouse-style bathrooms in an alley. The Hole in the Wall is the kind of place where guys anywhere from 21 to 80 can come for beer or whiskey or both and for man talk dominated by sports stats, outrageous stories, and *the-world-lacks-common-sense-and-is-going-to-hell-in-a-handbasket* themes. At times, the evidence that women exist is slim, save for the occasional female bartender and Courtney Love rasping over the speakers.

Indeed, the high testosterone levels can make JW appear like a crossover bar: receptive to both gay and straight, blue and white collar, bike and SUV, tourist and local. The Tipplers have witnessed all these demographics. Aside from rooting for the Saints, JW's also offers a Sunday refuge where D.C. transplants can safely admit to being Redskins fans. And for those who grow hungry during games, takeout from the newer, cleaner JW grill next door can be delivered to your stool.

Last but not least, for Bourbon Street, the Hole in the Wall's prices are mercifully low. Even the hard-pressed can afford to buy a round here. Quality drafts such as NOLA Golden Ale, Blue Moon, and Canebreak run four to five dollars, and Sunday-Thursday, bottles of Miller High Life are only two dollars. So it's not surprising to see the regulars settle into their stools for spans of two or three hours. Indeed, it's a wonder some guys ever leave.

Photograph by Gavin MacArthur

Name: Krazy Korner
Address: 640 Bourbon Street
Phone: 504-524-3157
Web site: www.krazykorner.com
Your tab: Three for one. Enough said.
What you're swilling: Cheap beer, well drinks, and, if you're not careful, tooters
What you're wearing: Bourbon Street T-shirt, your convention badge
What you're hearing: All '80s, all night
When you're there: Somewhere between the beginning and the end of your night
Tattoo themes: Not too many. The occasional barbed wire on the frat guys.
Your drinking buddies: Everyone from the convention, bachelorette partiers. It's a mixed bag of ages, though it skews a little older given the music played.
Best feature: Absolutely fantastic and talented cover bands

Everything about the pulsing, strobe-lighted Krazy Korner screams, *"Dance!"* The minute we walk in and hear "It's Been Such a Long Time," we hit the dance floor. Soon, we become the bread in an unexpected conventioneer sandwich, when a conference attendee scoots his way between us while we are distracted by "Don't Stop Believin'." We let him shimmy out his fantasy through "867-5309" and then move away. He waves happily and we, unsure whether to be offended or flattered by his bump and grind, choose flattered.

We groove through a full set of '80s greats delivered by the surprisingly talented band, Trick Bag, the prom band you wish you had. Parched, we head to the bar but are intercepted by scantily clad shot girls toting trays of tooters. Elizabeth wants one, but guest Tippler Lee nixes that idea, stating we lack sufficient cash. He might have been lying. One guy enjoys his "toot" with benefits. The shot girl holds the closed end of the tooter in her mouth while the guy takes the open end in his. Both dip into a pose that should only be done publicly in a yoga class. Eww. Losing our taste for a tooter, we scoot back to the dance floor, gyrating with conventioneers and other tourists to "Living on a Prayer."

When Trick Bag stops, so do we, heading up to the balcony for a breeze and a break. The balcony's three-for-one special yields a $6.50 tab for three Buds, a steal on Bourbon Street. We take our beers to the far side of the balcony and look up St. Peter towards Treme. It is a breathtaking view of Creole cottage roofs forming a patchwork slate quilt. In this moment of beauty, we hear the clarion call of Bourbon Street:

"Titties!"

Down the balcony stands a middle-aged man, decked in out-of-season Mardi Gras beads, joyfully screaming, "Titties!" He does not hold any of the beads over the balcony to lure nubile women into baring it all. Instead, after shouting his great yawp of "Titties!" he collapses onto his barstool in hysterical laughter. No one tells him to shut up or go to hell. No one responds at all, and that, we think, is the source of his delight. He is in a place that lets him gleefully announce to the world the thing he loves most, without shame or censure. New Orleans is a pretty tolerant city, but we all agree that if this guy leaned over an Uptown bar balcony with his wanton cry, he would be shuffled off by sober friends before he was arrested. But the French Quarter is one of the last places in the United States where, as long as you aren't hurting anyone else, you can say pretty much whatever you want, and loudly at that. It is a different kind of beauty than the timeworn slate roofs, but admirable nonetheless.

We return to the dance floor and "Jesse's Girl" and shake it for a few songs more, in the place where the only requirement is to be yourself and have fun. Titties, indeed.

Name: Le Boozé
Address: 300 Bourbon Street
Phone: 504-586-0300
Web site: www.sonesta.com/royalneworleans then select the dining and entertainment option
Your tab: Hotel prices for pretty standard drinks
What you're swilling: American beer, basic cocktails. The bartenders are competent and can fix a decent old fashioned, but this isn't the spot for high art.
What you're wearing: The suit you just ate dinner in, your team's jersey
What you're hearing: Lots of sports on the five TVs
When you're there: It's easier to see the people on the street during the day, but the show improves in the evening.
Tattoo themes: None we can see
Your drinking buddies: Fellow fans
Best feature: Endless bar and its view of Bourbon Street

Sometimes you end up at a bar because it's the closest door open. Such was the case for us with Le Boozé, a bar whose entire length runs parallel to Bourbon Street, giving patrons an unimpeded view of that busy stretch between Bienville and Conti. Set in the Royal Sonesta hotel, Le Boozé, a name only a drag queen could love, is a long, barely oval shaped bar that the Tipplers have walked by dozens of times, peered into, and dismissed as "touristy." Tonight it hosts neurosurgeons in town for a conference and a few attorneys logging continuing legal education hours, all watching baseball playoffs on the bar's numerous TVs.

The leather stools, dotted with brass nails, are comfy and we prop our feet on the brass rail, a touch we always appreciate, though Elizabeth grumbles at her $11 Maker's Mark. The lively crowd is full of Yankees haters who cheer when the Tigers polish them off. We ignore the TV for a better show: the Bourbon Street parade. Seated in a row next to the other patrons feels as if we are in a theater, watching the pageant unfold before us, with no idea of what's to come. We sit and watch a few minutes more, then join the action ourselves, taking our drinks with us, of course.

Name: My Bar
Address: 635 Bourbon Street
Phone: 504-267-71707-704-267-7170
Web site: www.mybar635.com
Your tab: Five to seven dollars per drink
What you're swilling: NOLA Golden Ale, Blue Moon, or the house specialty, a purple voodoo daiquiri
What you're wearing: Whatever you can dance in
What you're hearing: Zydeco and Cajun in the afternoon; rock or rhythm and blues in the evening. Like elsewhere on Bourbon, no cover.
When you're there: 4:00 P.M.–11:00 A.M.
Tattoo themes: None
Your drinking buddies: Tourists mainly, some locals
Best feature: Versatility. It is called My Bar, so have it your way—upstairs, downstairs, balcony, courtyard, different music genres, multiple flat screens, Saints games. Draft beer, full bar, daiquiris, and, of course, shooters are all offered in one human-sized space.

The band, a veteran rhythm and blues group, is on break, and without an emcee to keep the crowds from drifting out the door, My Bar is nearly empty when we and our guest Tipplers from San Francisco arrive. The customers are so sparse that the lone shooter girl has, in fact, given up. We settle on drafts of NOLA Golden Ale and choose a small table by the front doors over discreet conversation in My Bar's easy-to-miss back courtyard. We watch as across the street at Krazy Korner a man is placed in handcuffs while the band calmly plays Styx's "I'm Sailing Away." The upstairs bar is closed, but the room itself and the covered balcony are not. And like most of the bars with upstairs/downstairs arrangements, My Bar's look is a little more tasteful on the second floor, with decent chairs, a vintage mantel and mirrors, plastered walls, and a recently refinished bar.

But the dynamics change within a few minutes after the

band's return. The group launches into Kool and the Gang's "Ladies' Night," a song that happens to contain Allison's all-time favorite phrase, "sophisticated momma." And seeing her sway to the beat, a slim, elegant, blue-eyed lady, a sophisticated great-grandmomma, asks her to dance. By the end of the first number, several dozen customers have entered My Bar. The stools are full as the keyboardist leads the crowd through "Happy Birthday" and gives his best wishes to the lady with the 50 tiara on her head. And while this is not generally the case with My Bar, the average age tonight, including the band, hovers around 60.

The Tipplers are proud of the fact that our city, especially the Quarter, doesn't put an age cap on a good time. One of our guests, a music-show producer and someone who travels for her work a great deal, agrees. Unlike a lot of other cities she's visited where the bar scene is indeed a *scene* and therefore synonymous with twenty-somethings, New Orleans doesn't engage in de facto ageism. In the Big Easy, the more mature demographics are never made to feel as though they don't belong. It could be that with *so* many bars, patrons don't need to feel territorial and hedgy. But we think there's more to it than that. The French Quarter continues to draw people of all ages because it acknowledges a fundamental human need, and every time we wander through, there are plenty of silver foxes who demonstrate what the rest of the nation has been slow to learn. The desire to let loose never fades; it only gets more practiced.

Name: Old Absinthe House
Address: 240 Bourbon Street
Phone: 504-523-3181
Web site: www.ruebourbon.com/oldabsinthehouse
Your tab: Moderate, though the absinthe can be pricey
What you're swilling: Enjoy the show the bartenders put on when dripping the absinthe and flaming the sugar. The bloody mary is stellar.
What you're wearing: It's Bourbon Street. Expect to see about anything on the patrons.
What you're hearing: The roar of the street makes its way inside occasionally, but when the bar is empty, it is surprisingly quiet.
When you're there: It's easier to appreciate its charms when the bar is empty, so afternoons are nice.
Tattoo themes: We see a fleur-de-lis on our bartender, and most patrons have ink peeking out from under their shirts.
Your drinking buddies: Anyone who stumbles in from Bourbon Street, or trots (see below)
Best feature: The absinthe fountain from the 19th century is lovely, and if the bar's tour guide is available, take advantage of him to learn more of the history of the establishment.

Visitors to New Orleans often return home with tales of our "crazy city." These stories (always alcohol fueled) feature ill-considered or illegal acts: dancing obscenely, ogling naked bodies or displaying their own, and nursing crushing hangovers. And perhaps, in Dubuque, these actions are "crazy." But a better word that describes New Orleans, and the French Quarter in particular, is "magic." Magical moments abound here, though their visibility varies. Turning off your favorite electronic device and taking a long slow look around helps them come into focus. So does steady inebriation. But some magic requires nothing more than being in the right place at the right time, as the Tipplers are one evening at the Old Absinthe House.

There are bars in this city that never close, and then there are bars that feel as if someone has actually been drinking in them since the day they opened, almost 200 years ago. The Old Absinthe House wears the dull patina of a place whose doors have never been shuttered long enough to allow anyone to scrub away the sin. Elizabeth, who works nearby, has observed that someone is always drinking here, no matter the hour. One corner of the bar houses an original absinthe fountain, in place since the 19th century, when the Green Fairy flitted lightly among thirsty patrons. In anachronistic contrast to this historic artifact are the dozens of plastic football helmets hanging from the ceiling, giving the room a slightly decapitated air. We ignore the ceiling. Instead, we prop our feet on the vintage brass rail, hang our bags on the brass hooks under the bar, look straight ahead, and order our five-dollar whiskies.

It's a slow night, even for Bourbon Street, and our lone bartender moves from patron to patron with a practiced, steady tempo. When it's time for a refill, we barely raise our heads before she offers one. The TV is muted, the empty bar is quiet, so we scoot in to have a visit. The unmistakable smell of fresh popcorn wafts from the popper located across the bar, and we head over to claim a bowl. We are informed by the bouncer making the snack that the free popcorn will be delivered shortly to our seats. We return to our barstools to wait—and wait. The fragrant aroma fills the bar. The popper appears full, but, to our growing annoyance, no popcorn arrives. We take the popcorn delay personally, and our opinion of the Old Absinthe House darkens under a salty cloud. When the treat finally arrives, we joke that our popcorn fixation will be our story of the Old Absinthe House, a quaint anecdote in another night of quiet drinking in the French Quarter. We are, of course, mistaken.

Just as we are about to tuck into our popcorn, the bartender asks Allison and Richard to move over. About to ask why, we notice that she is no longer looking at us but looking up behind us. We follow her gaze and there, walking through the French doors, is a policeman sitting on his horse. The horse moves with the certainty of a regular and clops up to the bartender. Allison scoots over like a shot. The horse snuffles by Richard, aiming for the bartender's outstretched hand, which is full of maraschino cherries. He gobbles them up, but instead of backing away, he flares his nostrils, attentive to the delicious aroma of freshly popped popcorn. He buries his nose in Allison's snack, inhaling it in seconds. "Hey!" yells the bartender, as the cop pulls back on the reins. While the cherries are obviously a nightly treat, the popcorn is meant to be off limits. But that is news to the horse. Soon after, the horse and cop back out of the Absinthe House the way they came in, and we watch them trot off down Bourbon Street.

Good jokes and magical moments depend upon surprise. It is the unexpected ending that delights us. We decide to leave at the beginning of the joke: "A horse walks into a bar . . . "

Name: Old Opera House
Address: 601 Bourbon Street (at Toulouse Street)
Phone: 504-522-3265
Web site: www.oldoperahouse.com
Your tab: Ranges greatly
What you're swilling: Stoli and flavored Stoli, Malibu and Tequila Malibu, assorted shooters
What you're wearing: A black T-shirt that reads *bridesmaid* or *Megadeth*
What you're hearing: See below.
When you're there: Monday-Friday after 5:00 P.M.; Saturday and Sunday after 2:00 P.M.
Tattoo themes: Barbed wire
Your drinking buddies: Tourists
Best feature: Uplifting graffiti in the ladies' room

Act One

"Just a small-town girl . . . " sings the sharp-jawed, 30ish blond guy on stage. But apparently, the first line is as far as even this seasoned pro can get at the moment. After having sung Journey's "Don't Stop Believin'" each night (and perhaps more than once) for longer than should be inflicted on anyone—including Steve Perry—our singer appears to be experiencing a lapse of faith, despite the song's title.

Pointing the microphone in the direction of the audience and the smoke machine and scantily clad girls hawking neon test-tube shots, he bobs his head to the beat and yells out, "All right, you sing the rest!

Act Two

The *original* Opera House at the corner of Bourbon and Toulouse, also known as the French Opera, was a majestic theater built by famed New Orleans architect James Gallier in 1859. For decades, it played host to both trysts and formal Mardi Gras balls. Long considered the grandest building in the Quarter, the Opera burned—costumes, violins, and all—to the ground in 1919.

Across the street in a decidedly more modern era of Bourbon Street, the sopranos and symphonies of yesteryear have been replaced with a decidedly downsized five-piece cover band. But shows still run here nightly, and the audience knows the repertoire. And while opera scores have always been complex, the storylines aren't. Someone lives or dies tragically, gets the girl or no, wrestles with demons. The comparisons to "Jesse's Girl," by Rick Springfield, or Bad Company's "Can't Get Enough of Your Love" are clear.

"F@%★ yeah!" the singer erupts, *crescendo,* during the guitar solo.

Act Three

The band breaks after the Outfield's "Your Love." As the singer makes his way around the crowd with a tip jar, the Tipplers attempt an interview.

Q: Do you have a card?

A: There is no card.

Q: How to get in touch with you?

A: We're here every night starting at seven.

Q: Every night?

A: *Every* night.

Stage left: A young man wearing a Viking helmet sucks down a neon-green shooter with the help of the nearest waitress. A crew of khaki slacks and polo shirts ignore the blinking pagers attached to their belts. A bachelorette party raises its painted nails and wails, "*Woooo!*" A hefty middle-aged woman raises her phallic fleur-de-lis daiquiri container and impressively shakes her junk.

Act Four

One of the Tipplers' friends recently lamented that these kinds of establishments will be the only thing that some tourists remember about New Orleans. First, we're not so sure they *will* remember. But second, we're not so convinced that Bourbon is such a bad representative. If the spirit of a bar is embodied in its bathroom graffiti, then the Old Opera House must be positively edifying. Rather than the usual gamut of putdowns and vents, most of what the Tipplers discover is innocuous—a name and a date, testament to having passed this way. Others are surprisingly kind. *Have a great, creative life. Happy Mother's Day. I love everyone.*

Encore.

Photograph by Gavin MacArthur

Name: Tropical Isle
Address: 729 Bourbon Street
Phone: 504-529-4109
Web site: www.tropicalisle.com
Your tab: Depends on how many hand grenades you have and the decisions you make thereafter
What you're swilling: Probably a hand grenade but don't say we didn't warn you
What you're wearing: What you left the convention in, what your buddies abandoned you in
What you're hearing: A variety of live bands, mostly blues and rock and roll
When you're there: Weekend nights are the craziest, if that's your M.O.
Tattoo themes: Varies: some military tats, frat-boy barbed wire and tribal patterns, something more floral on the ladies
Your drinking buddies: Committed drinkers from around the globe, no locals
Best feature: The breathalyzer machine

It's Friday night. The hand grenade mascot dances in front of the bar, flirting with patrons as only a man in a hand grenade suit can. Tropical Isle is purportedly a Tiki bar but really looks like a high-school gym decorated for a prom whose theme is "Under the Sea." The ceiling is adorned with nets, sea creatures, and paper-mâché surfers getting nibbled by sharks. The bar smells slightly better than the last time we came and is full of drinkers clutching green plastic hand grenade containers. This drink will wreck you. That is its goal, and if you drink more than one, you should know that your likely destination is falling-down drunk.

We contemplate ordering the signature drink because why the hell not, but when we look around at how hammered everyone is, we decide to share one among the three of us. It is as cloyingly sweet as we all remember, so we switch to beer. The band churns out some classic rock, while patrons swing their hand grenades with a defiant determination "to get good and drunk."

Some visitors come to New Orleans for the food, some for the music, and some for the architecture. And some just come to get drunk and stay drunk as long as they want. If that's your primary reason to visit New Orleans, then Tropical Isle is your Mecca.

We're not saying that Tropical Isle is the only bar on Bourbon Street that encourages getting hammered as your main goal. There are three-for-ones up and down the street. But Tropical Isle promotes the hand grenade as the strongest drink on Bourbon Street—not the tastiest and not even the "best," just the one to put you over the edge the quickest. Also, Tropical Isle is the only bar of the 100 we list that includes a breathalyzer machine so that you can measure just how drunk you are. If Tropical Isle were a friend, he would be an enabler. But that's okay, because everyone deserves a friend like that, one who gives you permission to toss moderation out the window as you toss back another green demon. This may not be the Tipplers' favorite kind of drinking, but we recognize that the Quarter provides an important service to the rest of the United States, offering a space to test (and exceed) your limits without restraint or censure.

CHAPTER 3

Live-Music Bars

If any of our categories is self-explanatory, this is it. New Orleans has one of the best music scenes in the world, and nothing goes with music like booze. The Quarter offers enough venues that many professional musicians earn their entire living by working a few regular gigs here. And there is a real range of musical styles, including '80s cover bands, rhythm and blues, traditional jazz, indie rock, Zydeco, and everything in between. In most places, drinking, talking, and the music all coexist peacefully. So don't expect your fellow audience members to sit in respectful silence. In New Orleans, listening is an active verb. The one exception we can think of in this chapter is Irvin Mayfield's Jazz Playhouse.

The Quarter is a music Mecca because few spots charge covers, so don't feel as though you have to limit yourself to a single show. And better yet, you can take your drink with you as you walk to the next club. That said, not every music venue in the Quarter has made our Top 100. And some that have are listed elsewhere in the book, because music is only part of what they do. The Carousel Bar, for example, has plenty of live music, but to us, it's an iconic bar that happens to have music, not the other way around.

Belly up to the bar, shake a tail feather if you like, and for Pete's sake, don't forget to tip the band on your way out.

Name: Balcony Music Club
Address: 1331 Decatur Street (at Esplanade Avenue)
Phone: 504-599-7770
Your tab: Manageable. Generally speaking, prices drop the farther you get from Bourbon Street, and this is about as far as you can get and still be in the Quarter.
What you're swilling: We recommend beer, since you can shake your booty without spilling too much.
What you're wearing: Anything you can dance in
What you're hearing: Music and lots of it. It's loud. It's brassy. But it is also seriously good.
Tattoo themes: Ink abounds, but we haven't identified any particular themes. If you've got it, flaunt it.
Your drinking buddies: Mostly tourists but a few locals who've stopped in en route to Frenchmen Street, aka Bourbon Street for those of us who live here
Best feature: Stellar live music that you can hear from the street

It's Saturday night, and we're starting things off at the Balcony Music Club. It's a good choice: there's no cover, the bar's well stocked, and given its perch at the edge of the Quarter, it's very easy to reach (for locals, anyway). Richard arrives early and grabs a beer from the bar.

A brass band is warming up in the front room. Eager music lovers drift in to hear them play. Richard checks his e-mail and blows through a few levels of Angry Birds.

When he looks up again 15 minutes later, the place is packed. He can't even squeeze through to the pleasant courtyard, much less reach the balcony upstairs. He steps outside to wait for Elizabeth and Allison, who've been delayed. As usual, their dance cards are full.

When they do arrive, Richard pushes back through the crowd to grab a round of beer for all three. We consider wandering on, but the music is so good, why ruin a good thing? We lean against one of the balcony posts, enjoying the cool breeze.

Apparently, we look like the locals we are, because we're soon approached by a couple from out of town. "Excuse me," the woman says, "can you tell us the way to Bourbon Street?"

"Three blocks that way," Allison replies, pointing up Esplanade. "When you get there, make a left."

"What's good to do over there?" asks the man.

Richard responds hesitantly. The question might be completely innocuous, or the guy could be trying to pick all three of us up. It's hard to tell from his grin. "Well," Richard eventually says, "there are a lot of bars, if you like that sort of thing."

"What about music?" asks the woman. "Is there any live music?"

We glance quickly at one another, unsure if the woman can hear the brass band bellowing out beats just inside the club. Ever gracious and tactful, Elizabeth jumps in. "There is, but what you're hearing right now is at least as good—maybe better."

"Oh, thanks," says the woman, "but we're looking for real New Orleans music." And before we can respond, the couple sets off into the night, oblivious.

Name: Davenport Lounge
Address: 921 Canal Street (in the Ritz Carlton)
Phone: 504-524-1331
Web site: www.ritzcarlton.com
Your tab: $16 martinis. You do the math.
What you're swilling: Classic, well-made, expensive cocktails
What you're wearing: Classic, well-made, expensive togs
What you're hearing: Classic, well-made, expensive tunes
When you're there: After a great meal to enjoy some swinging jazz or earlier for a quiet visit
Tattoo themes: Not much ink in this classy joint
Your drinking buddies: Your fellow travelers, dinner companions, or law partners
Best feature: A sofa you could get lost in

The song "Puttin' on the Ritz" evokes opulence and splendor. Written by Irving Berlin in 1929, it is an homage to the swank style of the Ritz Hotel in London, whose properties now dot the globe. The New Orleans location easily delivers on these tony expectations, especially its bar, the Davenport Lounge. Though there are no "high hats and Arrowed collars" when we visit, it's clear that "lots of dollars" were spent in creating a lush, luxe space.

The Davenport Lounge, with its abundance of chintz and *objets d'arts,* belongs in your charming and wealthy godmother's manse. She's the kind of woman who loves 18th-century oil paintings and porcelain statues of both monkeys and milkmaids. The large open space is parsed into a dozen or so small groupings of extremely comfortable sofas and chairs, all flanked by side or coffee tables. These compositions form individual parlors conducive to intimate conclaves. In the low and benevolent lighting, we glow a rosy pink, though we haven't even tasted our first drink.

Our friend Barbara has recently secured a publishing contract for her book on historic perfumes, a worthy reason to splurge on the menu's $16 manhattans and martinis. Talk soon turns to perfumes of the 1920s, when women cut their hair and hems short. As a treat, Barbara pulls out a bottle of Lanvin's My Sin, and we sniff with interest. Her description is lavish. "My Sin is a sexual flower . . . like a meadow in full bloom visited by the horniest, healthiest bees. It smells lush, overripe, decadent." Though a fan of all perfumes, Barbara favors the early 20th century's scents, comparing the difference between modern and vintage perfumery to the difference between polyester and velvet. At this remark, Elizabeth pulls out a recent Etsy splurge, a 1930s compact with a well-crafted interior that is fit for engraving. The handsome compact, the heady perfume, the lush surroundings, and our extravagant cocktails transport us to a time of scintillating parties, when guests unleashed witticisms between sips of illegal hooch. While we appreciate our present era, where booze is legal and women can vote, we decide that past era had its own merits of quality and comfort.

The room swells with fans of the talented Jeremy Davenport band and the elegance rolls on, as Mr. Davenport croons Cole Porter's "I Get a Kick Out of You." The playlist won't take us farther than World War II, so we flag down our server and order another round. Tonight is not a time for restraint. Indeed, we are "spending every dime, for a wonderful time."

Photograph by John d'Addario

Name: Fritzel's European Jazz Pub
Address: 733 Bourbon Street
Phone: 504-586-4800
Web site: www.fritzelsjazz.net
Your tab: $10 cocktails; $7–8 beers. (Note: Fritzel's doesn't have a cover charge but does require one drink minimum per set.)
What you're swilling: Beer, whiskey and soda, bourbon
What you're wearing: Whatever you want; vintage always appropriate
What you're hearing: "When the Saints Come Marching In" and "St. James Infirmary Blues"; Fritzel's own compilation CDs featuring the regular acts available for sale
When you're there: Fritzel's claims to be the longest-running jazz club in the French Quarter (since 1969). Polished pros play "trad jazz" nightly starting at 9:00. Regular acts often span the generations, including both seasoned players and young bucks. Come earlier for regular drinking in the front bar or outside in the alley courtyard.
Tattoo themes: The gamut
Your drinking buddies: The world. During the Tipplers' latest visit, both Montreal and Omaha were in the house; Omaha looked a lot happier.
Best feature: Retro-ness, the combination of an intimate hole in the wall of exposed brick and arches erected in 1831 and the vintage swing that matches it

With its smooth traditional swing performances and raffish yesteryear charm, Fritzel's is largely geared towards tourists. And given the smiles from the packed-in crowd, it's safe to say that this bohemian hole in the wall is *exactly* what some tourists are hoping for when they come to New Orleans. It's not the kind of place locals are likely to frequent. However, this little club will always have a sentimental place in the Tipplers' hearts, for it offered us a set's worth of solace when we and our city were in a vulnerable state.

It was the Mardi Gras after Katrina. We had only been allowed reentry into the city the October before, and five months later our city was still in a fragile state for the biggest celebration of the year. The French Quarter was still intact and cleaned up in order to draw in the tourist trade, but beyond the Quarter waited a different story, with many neighborhoods or pockets in total ruin. "Devastation" bus tours were running a close second to the feel-good originals. More weighty than even the individual tragedies was an inescapable, unyielding collective sense of loss.

That year's Mardi Gras was for many a milestone, a psychological marker both of the start of a return to normalcy and a sign that we would survive as a city and a culture. In the weeks leading up to the celebration, as went about sourcing fabric and sequins, we all remember friends and neighbors saying, "Mardi Gras is the test. If we can put on Mardi Gras, we'll make it."

That year we went as a group costume, prophetically as cocktails—Allison as champagne, Elizabeth as a mint julep, Richard as a Pimm's cup. There was also a raw truth to those costumes. The months following the storm saw an immense amount of drinking, and while we know many would question the merits of that form of self-medication, it was what we had, and we stand by the way alcohol eased and numbed those months.

That Mardi Gras day, after making our way into the Quarter via the fabulously costumed St. Anne parade, we found ourselves (in the way that Mardi Gras often unfolds) in front of Fritzel's on Bourbon Street and in need of the relief trinity: shade, a bathroom, and a drink. The place was blessedly dark and uncrowded, and a swinging band was tooting on trumpets and oboes. We were miraculously able to find a table and stools. Elizabeth and Allison still recall dancing, twirling each other on the brick floor, and for the span of a set, the chronic weight of living in a devastated city was forgotten. For at least a little while, we were able to feel exactly what Mardi Gras had been created for and what had been nearly impossible since evacuation the previous August: abandon and joy.

Name: Funky Pirate
Address: 727 Bourbon Street
Web site: www.thefunkypirate.com
Your tab: Moderate if you stay away from the "specialty drinks"
What you're swilling: Beer is your cheapest bet, though the mixed drinks aren't too bad. Wine comes in airplane bottles.
What you're wearing: Whatever you've been walking around the Quarter in all day
What you're hearing: Blues, mostly (see below)
When you're there: There's fantastic music every evening, starting around 8:00 P.M. Plan your stop accordingly.
Tattoo themes: A variety
Your drinking buddies: Tourists, though not the average Bourbon Street crowd
Best feature: Awesome music

Just when you think you know a bar in the French Quarter, you get a surprise. We're out tonight with Gabi and Dan, Elizabeth's neighbors. Gabi, who has lived in New Orleans for about six years, has never been to the Funky Pirate. We prepare her, with prejudice: it's a tourist trap. The drinks will be expensive. Since it's a Tropical Isle affiliate, everyone will be hammered on hand grenades. The only up side will be the solid blues musicians who play here, and we expect to hear some soulful Elmore James and Junior Wells tunes in the midst of our sure-to-be touristy night.

We walk in to the sounds of Django Reinhardt and 1930s jazz, cranked out by the Hot Club of New Orleans, some of the most talented jazz musicians in town. So much for our musical prediction. This is the genre of music you hear at Fritzel's or Maison Bourbon, not the Funky Pirate, prompting Elizabeth to mutter, "What are they doing here?"

We walk in and the guitar player, Matt Johnson, recognizing Elizabeth, mouths, "What are you doing here?" Indeed, his question is just as relevant as hers, since most locals don't frequent this joint. We promise to explain at the break.

The aptly named Funky Pirate wins the prize as the most pirate-themed spot in the Quarter. In addition to the standard nautical touches of nets, anchors, and treasure, two mannequins dressed in ragged pirate togs lean and leer over the audience, and Capt. Jack Sparrow appears to be sitting in with the Country Bear Jamboree. A sign above the bar declares, "You can be a pirate" (if you weren't sure), and there you can buy a sword for $3.50 and an eye patch for even less. The Tropical Isle influence is also pervasive, with frozen drinks, peanuts, and condoms, all hand grenade flavored, available for purchase. Despite these cheesy surroundings, the patrons are low key, not the typical rowdy Bourbon Street throng, and appear to really enjoy the music, making requests throughout the set. Drinks are a little steep compared to some neighborhood bars ($4.25 for High Life) but not unreasonable for the stellar live music.

We visit with Matt during the set break, learning that Mondays are now jazz nights at the Pirate and that Hot Club has the gig through October. Gabi announces that she likes this spot and plans to visit on a future Monday. We agree and return to our stools, munching on our hand-grenade peanuts, swaying to Duke Ellington, and glad that Bourbon Street can still, sometimes, prove us wrong.

Name: House of Blues
Address: 225 Decatur Street
Phone: 504-310-4999
Web site: www.HouseOfBlues.com
Your tab: Moderate to low-pricey. It's not as cheap as some places we've named, but chances are good that you're watching an amazing show, so everything balances out.
What you're swilling: Depends on the band. Blues? Beer, obviously. Jazz? Maybe a cocktail? Emo? What does "maudlin" taste like?
What you're wearing: Match the crowd. If you're coming for a rock show, wear your best CBGB's vintage T. Hip-hop demands a little more style, a little more bling. If you're just stopping by for a drink at the restaurant bar, you have some flexibility.
What you're hearing: House of Blues (HOB) presents almost every kind of music in the book, and the preshow/intermission music varies accordingly.
Tattoo themes: All over the map. Feel free to show off what you've got, but it's going to have to be pretty awesome to compete with your bartender's ink.
Your drinking buddies: Depends entirely on the crowd. Like many bars in New Orleans, HOB has some 18+ shows, so the guy standing next to you sipping a soda may be younger than you're used to.
Best feature: We're big fans of HOB's smaller venue, dubbed the Parish. It and the courtyard both have a great, intimate vibe. We also like HOB's weekly gospel brunch, a variation on the traditional jazz brunch and a nice way to shake off Saturday night, no matter what deity you prefer (if any). There's nothing quite like belting out a few hymns while knocking back a round of mimosas.

So, this is what you're thinking: "Why would these guys (okay, two girls and a guy) review a chain joint like House of Blues?

In New Orleans, there's a bar on every corner—sometimes four per intersection—and that's not even counting the ones between stop signs. Couldn't they come up with some alternatives?"

The answer is simple: House of Blues boasts some of the best live music in the Quarter. Whether you're looking for rock, blues, electronica, or some magical hybrid version of the three, it's all here, under one roof. House of Blues is like a department store for concertgoers, but there's no layaway—or screaming kids, for that matter.

We're here to see Leslie Hall, a nouveau-disco oddity who hails from the cornfields of Ames, Iowa. She's known for her catchy beats, hilarious lyrics, and outrageous costumes, especially her collection of "gem sweaters," which look as if they were salvaged from "The Cosby Show"'s wardrobe department and subsequently bedazzled to hell and back. To Leslie's credit, they look a lot better on her than they ever did on Cliff and Clair.

The show is in a room called the Parish. It's adjacent to the big hall where House of Blues presents more mainstream fare, bands capable of drawing 1,000 eager fans in an evening. The Parish is tiny by comparison, with standing room for a couple of hundred people or so. But tipplers needn't worry: the Parish bar is just as well stocked as all the others on site. We belly up and order a round of Abitas to get things going.

The place isn't too crowded yet. Leslie is a late-night phenomenon, and it's barely nine o'clock. But the next time we look up from the bar, the room has filled, and people are shouting drink orders over our heads. No one asks us to move.

Before long, Leslie hits the stage, presenting the sort of low-rent, wacky performance that goes over really well in New Orleans. She and her backup dancers are sporting some crazy-looking jumpsuits, possibly of thrift-shop provenance, which look exponentially crazier because of the adorably goofy choreography. The crowd is completely into it. Students from Tulane and Loyola, gay men from the Quarter, and tourists who've wandered in from the street are getting down.

And then it's over. She sings her finale—the underground hit, "This Is How We Go Out"—and leaves the stage. The crowd lingers for a few minutes, then begins filtering out the door. We look at our watches and phones, wondering how it got to be so late. One of the nice things about seeing a great show in such a comfortable venue: time passes quickly.

Name: Irvin Mayfield's Jazz Playhouse
Address: 300 Bourbon Street (in the Royal Sonesta Hotel)
Phone: 504-553-2299
Web site: www.irvinmayfield.com
Your tab: $9-14 per drink
What you're swilling: Sazeracs, margaritas, champagne cocktails
What you're wearing: Upscale natty
What you're hearing: Jazz, from standards to contemporary and fusion
When you're there: Sunday-Tuesday after eight; Wednesday-Saturday after five
Tattoo themes: Too dark to know
Your drinking buddies: Tourists, locals, jazz aficionados
Best feature: The music. An impressive, regularly updated Web site posts the lineup. Wednesday-Saturday, multiple acts and sets each night; Sunday-Tuesday, shows go on at eight. Regulars include pianist Joe Krown and trumpeter Leon "Kid Chocolate" Brown; Tuesday often includes tributes to non-jazz greats such as the Beatles, the Grateful Dead, or Stevie Wonder. Also worth noting is the 11:59 Friday-evening slot offering local burlesque legend Trixie Minx.

Irvin Mayfield's Jazz Playhouse may sound self-explanatory, but it's worth remembering that this club was founded by the Grammy Award-winning trumpeter, composer, professor, and all around local overachiever. The Playhouse is all about jazz, and not the sort of chummy retro swing that you'll see at Preservation Hall or Maison Bourbon. This is a sizable, slick, dark lounge with serious jazz musicians and extremely expensive drinks in lieu of a cover charge (minimum one order per set). Quite simply, come here for the music and no other reason.

This sounds easier than it is. The French Quarter triggers the ADD that lurks within each of us. Those who come to the Quarter have a hard time sitting still; they have an even harder time being quiet and waiting *patiently* for drinks. For some, such experiences can feel like the adult version of detention. And in our experience, people *say* they like jazz more than they actually do. Perhaps they would like to think of themselves as the kind of people who can appreciate the complexities of jazz, only to find it requires a bit more effort than they thought. Tonight, as the Tipplers settle into a banquette at the back of the full room, the discrepancy between the myth and the reality is apparent at more than one candlelit table, including our own. Within the course of a set, a couple of Tippler beaus grow visibly *cranky*, even during an exceptional rendition of "St. James Infirmary Blues" by a rumpled, cantankerous old-timer pulled up to the stage and introduced as Mad Dog.

So tipplers beware: at Mayfield's club, jazz is taken seriously, and the music isn't *background* for flirting and chatting. Mayfield's isn't going to feel like a loose speakeasy. Of course, some don't require this warning—our apologies to the serious listeners. Here's a word to the wise. If you care about jazz, Mayfield's should be at the top of your list, but bypass the strained faces and sit as close to the stage as possible.

Name: Jimmy Buffett's Margaritaville
Address: 1104 Decatur Street (at Ursulines)
Phone: 504-592-2565
Web site: www.MargaritavilleNewOrleans.com
Your tab: Nothing you'll regret come Monday
What you're swilling: Take a guess.
What you're wearing: Visit Tommy Bahama and/or Chico's before dropping in or perhaps the Margaritaville shop just next door.
What you're hearing: Duh
Tattoo themes: Varied, but with an unusual number of cheeseburgers. (We kid; we kid.)
Your drinking buddies: Mostly tourists of a certain age, but they're all here to have fun, so don't judge
Best feature: Jimmy Buffett fans will insist that the main stage is the best part of Margaritaville, but we like the Storyville Tavern, where you're able to look out on one of the best blocks for drinking in the entire French Quarter. The Tire Swing bar upstairs is also a hit—provided you're sober enough to get into one of those swings with a drink in your hand. And the balcony is a great retreat once the sun goes down.

None of us are what you'd call Jimmy Buffett fanatics, but that doesn't matter at Margaritaville. This is a place for partying, whether or not you're a Parrothead.

Ordinarily, we'd mosey into the cavernous restaurant at the back of the building and order up some appetizers from the Caribbean-themed menu. But tonight, we're just resting for a few minutes between dinner (eaten elsewhere) and a party around the corner. We settle into the Storyville Tavern, Margaritaville's front bar. If it weren't for the guy strumming out rock ballads on his guitar, we might think we'd walked into a strip club. Perhaps that's because of the small stage off to the side, which feels slightly licentious (in a good way). Or perhaps it's because the bar is named for New Orleans' long-lost Storyville district, America's first experiment with legalized prostitution.

Strippers or no, this corner of Margaritaville turns out to be a great place to pause and regroup. The singer is pleasant but not overpowering. (Sorry, none of us remember his name.) And the crowd, though sparse, is enthusiastic but not Bourbon Street rowdy.

We order a round of bourbon—neat, please—and toast the night, hoping that it'll be a good one.

Name: Kerry Irish Pub
Address: 331 Decatur Street
Phone: 504-527-5954
Web site: www.kerryirishpub.com
Your tab: Five to six dollars per drink
What you're swilling: Guinness, Maker's Mark
What you're wearing: Something comfy
What you're hearing: Live music seven nights a week—rock and roll, traditional Irish, originals
When you're there: After nine
Tattoo themes: Fleur-de-lis, Celtic knots
Your drinking buddies: Regulars, locals, some tourists
Best feature: Devoted regulars, both drinkers and musicians

With no shortage of Irish bars in the Quarter, it's inevitable that some feel more Irish than others. Sometimes a clover or flag isn't enough to make a bar feel *authentic*. Kerry Irish Pub, however, feels genuine. Though not upscale, it manages to look a little more put together than most of the Irish bars in the Quarter. Framed prints of the Emerald Isle's famous exports as well as of musicians hang on exposed-brick walls. A heavy, scarred wooden bar dominates the front while a small stage, pool table, and dartboard fill the back. Cigarette smoke clouds the air. On the ceiling, dollar bills, most marked with names and dates, attest to the hundreds who have passed over Kerry stools.

This quixotic record of human existence continues into the ladies' bathroom, where a chaotic sprawl covers the walls and ceiling. Some of the messages date back a decade—names, places, philosophical statements, and vents from the recently dumped or betrayed. Perhaps our favorite is the terse, considered pronouncement of this anonymous writer: *I love Scott, but would rather spend the rest of my life with James.*

A visitor looking carefully can spot small brass plaques mounted on the outside edge of the bar. They're engraved *reserved for* and then the name of a Kerry regular. It's an honor that can't be bought, only awarded by the owners. It's the Tipplers' luck that on this Saturday night, we're sitting next to one of the engraved—a local, semiretired printmaker who in his day saw Woodstock, Jimi Hendrix, the Rolling Stones, and Joni Mitchell. In the tradition of a real Irish pub, where neighbors of all generations intersect, we fall into easy conversation.

Indeed, Kerry mainstays are the locals, those who have lived in New Orleans long enough to sink roots and who come into the pub enough to know which bartenders work which shifts and when the band has changed its set list. Certainly their investment is another reason why the Kerry feels true to the Irish tradition. When we ask our new friend why he chooses the Kerry as his watering hole, he immediately says the people. He knows them and considers them family, including those now late for their set. It's also clear that our regular is generous in welcoming newcomers into the fold. Even though the Tipplers are visiting together, we could have come alone and never been made to feel it.

Without the distraction of a room crammed with televisions, we spend a round in effortless talk as we wait for the band. Finally the guitar player arrives, and our new friend teases him that he's an hour late. There's a smile, a shrug, some handshakes all around, and a little banter, and we learn that Krazy Korner, where he plays the afternoon set, is his bread and butter. Finally the group takes the stage and launches into its first number, a low-key rock-and-roll original. And even so, like a genuine pub, the music at the Kerry doesn't drown out the human connection: talk.

Name: Maison Bourbon
Address: 641 Bourbon Street
Phone: 504-522-8818
Web site: www.maisonbourbon.com
Your tab: Moderate; minimum one drink per set
What you're swilling: The bar can get really crowded and loud. It's best to keep your order simple.
What you're wearing: Nothing too risqué, though T-shirt and shorts are fine.
What you're hearing: Traditional New Orleans jazz, jazz standards
Tattoo themes: None
Your drinking buddies: Fellow jazz fans
Best feature: Fantastic music

A wedding photographer once told Elizabeth that the hardest part of his job is that he's at work while everyone around him is at a party. We imagine it must be that way to play on Bourbon Street. Even if you are aware of your good fortune to make a living doing what you love, some nights the job must feel like, well, a job. It doesn't matter if you are sick, tired, or hung over, you can't hide behind your desk and you can't be in a bad mood when the audience is expecting you to entertain them. Fortunately, tonight at Maison Bourbon, trumpeter Jamil Sharif and his band look anything but stale.

An usher leads us to three empty seats by the bar on a packed Thursday evening. Sharif has just started his set, and we order our beers to the blare of "All of Me." Portraits of past acts, all clad in the same 1970s ruffled tuxedo shirt and all wearing the same grin, seem to be enjoying themselves as much as the guys on stage.

Tonight, we are treated to the smooth collaboration of musicians who have been playing together for years. Sharif and his saxophone player easily trade riffs before tossing it back to an aged piano player who looks a bit like Rowlf the Dog from "The Muppet Show" as he hunches over his keys.

The band starts "In the Mood," and after solos make their way around the stage, Sharif starts playing more and more quietly, slowly sinking down to his knees. The band follows his lead and soon they are all leaning down, the saxophone practically touching the floor, the piano player prone across the ivories, while the drummer has abandoned his set and is barely tapping the edge of Sharif's trumpet. Then they are so quiet we cannot hear them, and for a few moments, they play only for each other. The audience delights in observing the genuine pleasure these artists take from their work.

Then, with a quick swoop of his trumpet, Sharif raises his musicians. The lull is broken, the volume soars, and we are all lifted on a swinging flight.

CHAPTER 4

Neighborhood Bars

New Orleans takes pride in its dozens of neighborhood bars. Unlike some cities, where you have to get in a car and drive to the nearest watering hole, in New Orleans, you can usually make the trip on foot. In fact, thanks to our lax booze laws, you can fix a cocktail at home and make the stroll to your local pub, sipping all the way.

While the Quarter as a whole caters to tourists, people do live and work here. As a result, a small but reliable crew frequents the saloons located across from their workplaces or houses. There, you'll see patrons grouped in corners, gossiping about local events and, of course, other residents.

By their very nature, neighborhood bars are not fancy. These are whiskey-and-soda or beer kinds of places. Here you can feel comfortable drinking alone, and the music isn't so loud that you can't talk with friends.

Going to a neighborhood bar is one of the best ways to learn what it's like to live in a given locale, so if you want a peek behind the French Quarter curtain, our neighborhood bars will provide it.

Name: Boondock Saint
Address: 731 St. Peter Street
Phone: 504-525-4950
Your tab: Five dollars for decent beer
What you're swilling: Something Irish
What you're wearing: T-shirt and shorts
What you're hearing: Classic rock from the jukebox
When you're there: Late afternoon-night
Tattoo themes: Tribal, floral
Your drinking buddies: Buddies, pirates, possibly cops
Best feature: Normalcy so close to Bourbon

The Boondock is located on a stretch of the Quarter that is particularly dense with drinking establishments. Just half a block from Bourbon, we can hear bars such as Krazy Korner already pumping out Journey and Pat Benatar covers. Meanwhile, a steady, or perhaps not so steady, stream of tourists clutches green grenades and rustles with beads. And it's not even night yet. Directly across the street, a more sober looking line for Preservation Hall stretches down the sidewalk despite the deep sweats of July. A late-afternoon thunderhead threatens to break overhead. With so much action, it can be easy to miss the Boondock's slim entry and green shutters. This discretion is also why the Boondock remains popular among those seeking asylum from Bourbon Street.

The Boondock belongs to a surprisingly plentiful category in the Quarter—the self-identified Irish bar. But step inside and you'll see it belongs to what might be called the shiver-me-timbers style of French Quarter bars—a fairly common look with heavy, dark-brown wood beams and walls evoking the hull of a pirate ship. The Boondock's narrow and long proportions only add to the boatlike feel.

Indeed, as the Tipplers take stools along the long bar, we notice a robust man dressed as a pirate—or as we locals say, "privateer"—sitting at the other end. It doesn't appear to be a happy day on the high seas. He sits alone, gripping a mug of beer and glaring, as if provoking us to say something disparaging about his headscarf. Of course, it's fairly common to see a swashbuckler or vampire (after the sun sets) downing a pint in the Quarter. No doubt our grumpy privateer is among the ranks who earn their living by giving themed night tours or performances. This evening, he appears to be reconsidering his vocation. We do not ask if he is an *Irish* pirate.

The bartender, a young curly blonde, asks us if it's to go, not surprising so near Bourbon. But those who stick around get glassware. The lady Tipplers order what has become a mainstay at neighborhood bars, whiskey and soda, while the gents opt for half-and-halfs from the Guinness and Harp on tap. Lifting their eyes to the three televisions overhead, the men discuss the new Hornets lineup as the jukebox moves from '80s English pop into an interminable string of early Billy Joel hits.

At four to six bucks a drink, the Boondock is cheap enough to stay for several rounds and exudes the kind of immediately familiar vibe of neighborhood bars: the dollar bill taped over the register, the Jägermeister station, the stack of potato-chip bags just waiting for your resolve to give out. It's easy to settle in and people watch or debate important things such as which Billy Joel album came *third*. And so it takes a while for the Tipplers to look up and spot the dozens of sheriff and patrol patches from across the country tacked to the beams overhead. Thieves and pickpockets be warned.

As the Tipplers discuss ordering another round, our sneering privateer is suddenly off his stool. Standing in front of the mirror by the door, he reaches into his leather saddlebag and withdraws a black tricorne hat. He takes his time adjusting the angle of his brim and examines his swarthiness from the front and side. Finally satisfied, he grips his wooden sword and steps out into the street.

Name: The Chart Room
Address: 300 Chartres Street
Phone: 504-522-1708
Your tab: So very cheap
What you're swilling: Beer and well drinks
What you're wearing: Anything more than a thong and you're good
What you're hearing: New Orleans greats from the jukebox
When you're there: Anytime, but we love late afternoons
Tattoo themes: All kinds
Your drinking buddies: Lots of locals
Best feature: All the overheard New Orleans accents

A cop once told Elizabeth that he loved the Chart Room because it offered Metairie prices in the Quarter. But there's more to love here than cheap booze. Instead, locals (and tourists who pass for locals) pack the dim pub because it feels like New Orleans: welcoming, insouciant, and worn. They come for a jukebox boasting iconic local names: James Booker, Fats Domino, and Irma Thomas, joined by newer performers such as Kermit Ruffins, Trombone Shorty, and Anders Osborne. That New Orleans sound greets the Tipplers as we enter the Chart Room one sleepy twilight. We have just left the posh environs of the Hermes Bar, where we sipped on happy-hour champagne, but the Chart Room beats even happy-hour prices. James Booker wails out "St. James Infirmary Blues" as we snag a prime table adjacent to the French doors. This is a favorite spot in the Chart Room, and Elizabeth claims the chair right next to the door, sitting so near the sidewalk that at one point in the evening, she gestures wildly and grazes a pedestrian.

There's no table service, so we send envoys to the bar. And there, too, are the sounds of New Orleans. The bartender and most of the patrons seated there speak in that slow drawl called "Yat," more Brooklyn than Southern.

Though we know the prices will be low, they remain a

pleasant surprise: draft High Life for $2 and a "mostly-gin" gin and tonic for $3, all cash, please. The tiny bill promotes acts of benevolence. Rounds are bought. Tabs are fought over: "No, let me get that." It's easy to be generous at the Chart Room, and in this credit-card-driven world, it feels lavish to pull out cash to pay for friends' drinks, even if all you need is a 10.

We wait for our drinks near a series of benches lined up along the wall, their seats worn from the thousands of bums that have settled into their valleys for a long night of drinking. Thoughtfully placed hooks above the benches (the better to squeeze in more bodies) boast Saints and LSU baseball caps, confirming a very local clientele. The sports theme continues in the several dozen pennants that have been hanging here since at least 1979, as evidenced by the New Orleans Jazz Basketball ensign.

The jukebox switches to Fats Domino, a perfect soundtrack to a night of drinking in NOLA. As the day darkens, our table livens, and at these prices it seems absurd to drink elsewhere. We stay put in that space, seated half in the bar, half out, our laughter mingling with Kermit Ruffins into the perfect New Orleans sound.

Name: Club Tango
Address: 300 Burgundy Street
Phone: 504-525-8775
Your tab: Three to six dollars per drink
What you're swilling: Miller High Life, Hennessy, vodka, mini-bottles of Freixenet (see special below)
What you're wearing: It's all good.
What you're hearing: "Soul Train" memory lane from the jukebox—Funkadelic, Parliament, Tower of Power
When you're there: During happy hour #1 (4:00-7:00 P.M.) or happy hour #2 (1:00 A.M.-close) for two-dollar Miller High Life bottles
Tattoo themes: All kinds
Your drinking buddies: Regulars, young punks
Best feature: Jukebox

For a city with such a large African-American population, there are almost no Afro-centric bars in the Quarter. Suffice it to say, New Orleans remains, in many ways, a divided city. By its own definition, Club Tango is a neighborhood bar, catering both to the Quarter and, given the bar's location on the edge of the Vieux Carré, to the nearby Tremé, America's oldest black neighborhood. With its small scale, cheap drinks, red lights, security cameras, and bathroom key, little Club Tango certainly qualifies as a dive as well and one that can attract some tourists. But the Tipplers agree that its business is drawn from the surrounding blocks, and local flavor is what most defines the atmosphere and decor.

When we arrive, the bar is nearly empty, but Funkadelic is playing over high-end speakers, perhaps the best we've heard, and a projection screen is showing a BET reality show. Our bartender projects the friendly but cool vibe of the 1970s. We like him instantly. He says the bar's busiest hours are after midnight.

Upscale-beer drinkers be forewarned: Club Tango doesn't

do microbrews, not even the local Abita. The usual American suspects are in order here. Aside from that, there's a substantial vodka selection and a few stray liquors such as Captain Morgan, Jack Daniel's, and Hennessy. The drink menu on a wall-mounted vinyl banner makes the price range clear: except during the happy hours, everything at Club Tango is $3-6, including call drinks. It also offers what we're willing to go on record as calling the Quarter's only *Champagne and Pig Lips and Chips* special. Granted, the champagne is a mini-bottle of Freixenet, the lips are from the jar on the counter, and the Zapp's jalapeno chips aren't hand-crafted. Nevertheless, at $6, it's worth noting that Club Tango's version remains exactly $84 cheaper than the similarly themed special—Veuve Cliquot and Frites—at Sylvain.

Name: Cosimo's Bar
Address: 1201 Burgundy Street (at Governor Nicholls Street)
Phone: 504-522-9715
Your tab: You'll have plenty left over for that cab ride home.
What you're swilling: Keep it simple: beer and bourbon are the stars here.
What you're wearing: This is the sort of place people visit after work to take the edge off. A few may be in suits, but most will be much more casual.
What you're hearing: Radio-style music played at manageable levels, to accommodate conversationalists
Tattoo themes: None per se, but given the very local clientele—especially the high number of service-industry personnel—don't be surprised if you come across some very good, very expensive ink
Your drinking buddies: Folks from the neighborhood, with few if any tourists
Best feature: Cosimo's is one of the most "local" bars on our list. If you want to get a feel for what makes an authentic New Orleans neighborhood bar, this is a great place to start your research. (And the food here ain't too bad, either.)

We've just slipped out of a party on Esplanade Avenue, and we're dressed to the nines. It's Carnival season, so naturally we're covered in glitter. One of us is wearing a cape. He has asked to remain nameless.

One block into our walk, Elizabeth realizes that—horrors!—she left the party without a beverage in hand. Luckily, Cosimo's is nearby to remedy the situation. Opening the door, we feel slightly out of place—and by "slightly" we mean "completely." Everyone at the bar looks as if they've just gotten off work. No one gives us any odd looks, but we're clearly not in step with the rest of the clientele.

Thirty minutes and a cocktail-and-a-half later, we're feeling much better. Another friend who'd been at the party walks in, his lapel covered in dollar bills. His birthday doesn't technically start until midnight, but he's not shy about getting a head start.

Another half-hour passes. We're supposed to meet friends at a different bar several blocks away, but we're comfortable, and we're having a good time, so we text them and tell them to join us here. When they do, one of them orders a celebratory round of shots.

The rest of the night is a blur. According to reports, Richard gets into a fiercely competitive game of pool in the back room. And two of our friends—well, let's just say they've been together ever since.

Cosimo's may not have the party vibe of Bourbon Street, but if you bring your own party, you won't notice a bit.

Name: Erin Rose
Address: 811 Conti Street
Phone: 504-523-8619
Web site: www.erinrosebar.com
Your tab: Pretty cheap unless you splurge on aged whiskey
What you're swilling: Something Irish: coffee (hot or frozen), whiskey, beer
What you're wearing: Something comfortable—you may be here a while
What you're hearing: Whatever is rotating on the jukebox, probably local
When you're there: Day or night, possibly both
Tattoo themes: Sailor themes are popular, and pin-ups on both the girls and boys
Your drinking buddies: Locals and visitors alike, with lots of other bartenders after 3:00 A.M.
Best feature: The superfriendly bartenders and the joie de vivre of the bar itself

At the Erin Rose, there's no need to wait for the weekend to enjoy weekend drinking. Maybe your service-industry job keeps you busy then, or maybe you got laid off, so now every day is Saturday. Their "Wake Up and Live" specials, offered daily from 10:00 A.M. to 2:00 P.M., include three-dollar mimosas and screwdrivers. The Tipplers duck into the Erin Rose one Wednesday afternoon to escape a summer shower, just in time to "wake up and live." Allison and Elizabeth toast staying dry with mimosas, while Richard splurges on a shot of 12–year-old Jameson. The Erin Rose pours all things Irish, including Bushmills, Guinness, Harp, and several years' worth of Jameson. We all listen approvingly as someone plays Dr. John on the jukebox, a slow soulful tune that matches the wet weather.

Though the walls and ceiling are covered with typical neighborhood-bar paraphernalia (hundreds of patron photos, newspaper articles, flags, blowup dolls, and signs both geographic

Photograph by John d'Addario

and political), the defining architectural feature of "the Rose," as locals call it, is the bar itself. It stretches the length of the room and almost fills the entire space, allowing just enough margin for patrons to shimmy behind the stools to make their way to the jukebox or back bar, where you can order gourmet sandwiches from Killer Poboys.

Soon we tuck into a Jameson grilled cheese and merguez po' boy, as our exuberant bartender, Mollie, refills our glasses, greets new arrivals, makes dinner and tour recommendations, and shares a shot with a patron seated down the bar. The bar transforms into the table of a good friend's house, a fitting tribute to the Rose's founder, Jim Monaghan, a true French Quarter character. Jim launched the French Quarter's St. Patrick's Day parade and the Krewe du Vieux parade, a vulgar confection that careens through the Marigny and Quarter during Carnival. He ran for City Council on the slogan, "What the French Quarter needs is asses on chairs."

But the role he most fully embraced was that of publican and host. He passed away in 2002, but his spirit lives on in the easy, affable vibe of the Erin Rose. Jim's ashes sit by the cash register, while his photograph above the bar smiles down approvingly on the convivial scene. Hanging next to his image is a massive drugstore sign for *Prescriptions,* an apt symbol in a place that aims to cure whatever may ail you with a shot and a smile. It's easy to drink here, at 3:00 P.M. or 3:00 A.M., alone or with friends. We tell ourselves we're waiting for the storm to stop, but even when the sun comes out blazing, we don't budge from this snug, dry, genial spot.

Name: Fahy's
Address: 540 Burgundy Street
Phone: 504-586-9806
Your tab: Low
What you're swilling: Irish is best.
What you're wearing: Anything goes.
What you're hearing: Mixed bag of tunes from the jukebox
When you're there: After your shift, on your day off, and when your billiard or dart club is playing
Tattoo themes: All kinds
Your drinking buddies: Service-industry employees, dart- and billiard-club players
Best feature: The service-industry pole of defiance

"The third place" is a term coined by sociologist Ray Oldenburg in his book *The Great Good Place*. Our first place is home and our second is work, but third places vary widely, including cafes, churches, diners, bookstores, and, of course, bars. Though these locales differ in their aims, all offer fellowship, solace, and refuge from life's difficulties. The Tipplers' favorite kind of third place is, of course, a bar, in particular a neighborhood bar such as Fahy's.

As Irish bars go, Fahy's seems more Irish than most, displaying both a large map of Ireland and a framed proclamation from the Provisional Government of the Irish Republic. All other wall space houses dartboards for the Fahy's dart club's weekly tournaments, though tonight the bar is packed with the billiard club.

After placing our standard Irish-bar orders of whiskey and Guinness, we take a seat, noting a pole at one end of the bar covered in squares of fabric. The several dozen squares are pieces of chefs' coats bearing a restaurant monogram. Their jagged edges suggest they were violently ripped from the jackets, and many bear dates scrawled across them.

We ask about the pole, and the bartender informs us that several years ago, the head chef at the restaurant catty-corner to the bar regularly hired cooks from South America to work in his restaurants on temporary visas. The chef was allegedly, ahem, "difficult to work for." His foreign cooks were unable to seek other work because their visas were tied to his restaurant, so after every shift, they would head over to Fahy's to commiserate.

One night, after one cook had finished his "indentured servitude," he came into the bar and ripped off the logo from his coat, swearing he "wasn't wearing that damn name for one minute more." He asked for a stapler. Then, in an action echoing Martin Luther nailing *The Ninety-Five Theses* to the church door, he impaled the badge onto the pole with a determined whack. What started as a means to voice a workingman's unhappiness became a tradition, though now that the chef has moved on, people affix other monograms with their names added but without the spirited message behind them.

We toast the pole, a fantastic, defiant "screw-you" to lousy bosses everywhere. We also toast Fahy's, a refuge to anyone who's had to endure unfair employers. A pole like that can only be created in a place where you feel totally safe, in a sanctuary from oppression—in your third place.

Name: Flanagan's
Address: 625 St. Philip Street
Phone: 504-598-9002
Your tab: Cheap
Web site: www.flanagans-pub.com
What you're swilling: Guinness on tap; Jameson neat
What you're wearing: Whatever you want
What you're hearing: Your fellow barflies visiting with each other
When you're there: Pretty much anytime, but the crowd picks up after midnight
Tattoo themes: Sailor, pin-up, fleur-de-lis
Your drinking buddies: Service-industry personnel drinking pre- or postshift
Best feature: The square bar and the movies sometimes shown on the screen in the back

Flanagan's is a great French Quarter neighborhood bar, and not just because every time we go, we see someone we know. Despite the bar being the meeting point for a New Orleans Haunted History tour, its clientele is standard Quarter Rat. Folks here, on their way to or from work in the service industry, favor white T-shirts and Buddy Holly frames but without the hipster self-awareness. That's because there's nothing really cool here; instead, everything is cozy.

The ceiling beams are wide, dark, and low and create an atmosphere that evokes an East Coast whaling tavern. You half-expect to see some grumpy pirate or drunken sailor in the corner. In the next room is a long wooden table, about the size you find in a junior-high-school cafeteria, big enough to accommodate a rugby team or, in tonight's case, the Noisician Coalition, a band composed of people who make their instruments from found objects. They are planning their Voodoo Fest gig, having come a long way from their early informal parades through the French Quarter and Ninth Ward following Hurricane Katrina. We wave to our friend, Elizabeth Zibilich, their Executive Minister of DisInformation, but she is too engrossed in sorting out logistics to visit. We leave her to discussions of instrument repair and uniform styles and take a seat at the square bar in the middle of the room. Its design allows for plenty of seating and visiting with our friendly barkeep.

Though its name indicates otherwise, Flanagan's is not really an Irish place. There is little decor that would set it apart from any other neighborhood pub, unless you count the full set of the 1968 edition of the *Encyclopedia Britannica,* which is available for anyone who needs to look up something since iPhone service in the Quarter is terrible. Still, we each order a Guinness, because it's on tap and because it goes well with the shot of Jameson that Elizabeth has a hankering for. The bartender is friendly and serves us quickly, but since it's a slow Tuesday night, he resumes chatting with his friend at the other end of the bar. Their discussion, which centers on a banana-bread recipe gone awry, seems incongruous with their full sleeves of tattoos, but really, who doesn't love banana bread? The bartender laments, "It just didn't taste as good as my mom's, even though I got her recipe." "I know, dude, I know. That's what happens," his companion sanguinely affirms. They punctuate the moment of disappointment with a shared shot. While most of the liquor sits across from the beer taps, the bottle of Bulleit stays perched by the Guinness, and the bartender shares an occasional snoot-full when familiar customers arrive.

Elizabeth's first date with Lee was here, a good choice. Flanagan's is not too loud or expensive, so you can talk into the night (and morning) without worrying about your tab. While the setting is dark, it's not a total dive. Flanagan's is what bars were intended to be: a gathering place, where you aren't competing with a jukebox or TV or band, a place to visit with old friends or a new love.

Name: Harry's Corner Bar
Address: 900 Chartres Street
Phone: 504–524–1107
Your tab: Cheap
What you're swilling: Beer, the standards, and their bloody marys are reliable
What you're wearing: LSU and Saints gear; nothing fancy
What you're hearing: Good New Orleans standards from its solid jukebox
When you're there: Saints and LSU games are a ton of fun here, though nights are lively too
Tattoo themes: Old-school tats from the '50s and '60s
Your drinking buddies: Your neighbors in the Quarter
Best feature: The local vibe

"Where y'at?" is New Orleans slang for "How are you?" It distinguishes residents whose broad Brooklynese accents mark them as "Yats" from other citizens. There's no standard definition for a Yat, but the ideal example was born in a New Orleans working-class neighborhood and attended a Catholic high school, though not the highest echelon of that category. When the Saints were bound for the Super Bowl, Yats prayed to the Blessed Mother for a win. Yats don't leave to go skiing during Mardi Gras, and most belong to a midlevel Carnival krewe. They have strong opinions about who makes the best gumbo and po' boys. They are fiercely loyal to their city and its traditions, to the point of being suspicious of newcomers. They might be rabid LSU fans, but there is no way in hell they would ever consider living in Baton Rouge.

Of all the bars in the French Quarter, Harry's Corner Bar is the Yattiest. Why? Well, let's start with the bartender. If you've been drinking around the French Quarter as steadily as we have, you notice that its bartenders skew young. Slinging drinks in Booze Central is hard work, requiring the stamina to handle a busy crowd until sunup. Though the image of a typical American bartender may be Mo from "The Simpsons," you don't see guys his age working behind the bar much in the Quarter. He greets us with a welcoming smile when we walk in, lays down some napkins, and asks what he can get us. We order three drinks, and when we tell him we will pay for them "all together," he rolls his eyes and declares that is "too much math" and he'll "have to take off my shoes to add that high." We chuckle at the joke, then grin at the price: $12, cash only, for two beers and a tasty bloody mary.

We're here tonight with Elizabeth's neighbors, Gabi and Dan. Harry's was the first bar Gabi ever visited in New Orleans. Her hotel was "somewhere nearby," and Harry's was the closest watering hole. Her memory of the night is fuzzy, but she does remember thinking how different Harry's was from what she imagined New Orleans would be. She expected Bourbon Street (which she hit the next night) but instead found a neighborhood bar where she felt like a local.

The bar is festooned with banners for LSU and the Saints and is crammed with dozens of patrons and at least two dogs clad in purple-and-gold LSU jerseys, waiting for the LSU kickoff. Harry's is dog friendly, and a sign near the door urges patrons to keep both their dogs and husbands on a tight leash. Fans greet each other, asking, "How's ya momma 'n' 'em?" Someone's "go, Tigers!" earns a "yeah, you right!" Snippets of conversation drift towards us. There's concern about the Saints' defense this season. We hear recommendations for a good roofer and a reminder that the last day for post-Hurricane Isaac debris removal is Monday. Two ladies, sipping Taaka, discuss the merits of Avon's new skincare line. "It's for your wrinkles, hawt."

We take our drinks outside to the bench under the window. Dan laments that his favorite outside table is now gone: a circular piece of plywood with a hole cut in it that fit snugly over the fire hydrant on the corner. He wonders if someone stole it. Richard thinks the fire department probably removed it, murmuring something about "codes." Sigh.

We decide to move along, leaving space for other LSU fans to congregate, toasting their brimming cups with cries of "ya heard!"

Photograph by Gavin MacArthur

Name: Johnny White's
Address: 733 St. Peter Street
Phone: 504-523-0839
Web site: www.johnnywhitesfrenchquarter.com
Your tab: Low
What you're swilling: Draft beer and shots
What you're wearing: Harley Davidson T-shirt, leather
What you're hearing: New Orleans classics from the jukebox
When you're there: It's open 24 hours, so whenever you need it.
Tattoo themes: Soooo many tattoos—eagles, ladies, names, ladies' names, skulls, sea creatures
Your drinking buddies: Fellow bikers; anyone in for the long haul of drinking in the wee hours
Best feature: Often quiet, it's a dark and undemanding contrast to Bourbon Street a half a block away.

Johnny White's is our second stop on our St. Peter stroll, an evening when we decide to confine all of our drinking to one block. However, the challenge to achieving that goal is finding the fortitude to rise from one barstool and shuffle off to the next one. Of all the bars we visit that night, Johnny White's is the hardest to leave.

It is a bar that has been open for almost 50 years, and we mean that literally. Johnny White's is a 24-hour bar that is filled with a haze that comes from decades of patrons' steady drinking and smoking. The decor is the eclectic but recognizable style we have dubbed "French Quarter Neighborhood Bar." The walls are covered with anything that will stick: hundreds of photos of patrons and bartenders, Saints paraphernalia both aged and new, and a mounted deer head adorned with the symbols of the season. Today he wears a Saints jersey and cap, but we are told that his Halloween garb is eminent.

We visit with our bartender, who has been pouring drinks at Johnny White's for 10 years, and ask him about his clientele. He acknowledges that Johnny White's is sometimes a biker bar, but those folks aren't the only patrons by any means. Its late hours make it popular among service-industry workers. Its history keeps it firmly entrenched among Quarter dwellers as a neighborhood bar. Its proximity to the madness that is the intersection of St. Peter and Bourbon makes it a popular stop for tourists. Its low prices make it a spot where the Tipplers want to park themselves for the night. Johnny White's is the only stop that night where we have two rounds, breaking our rule to move along with each drink. We're certainly not the first to keep sitting here, regardless of our best intentions. We won't be the last.

Name: Molly's at the Market

Address: 1107 Decatur Street (between Ursulines and Governor Nicholls)

Phone: 504-525-5169

Web site: www.MollysAtTheMarket.net

Your tab: Not dirt cheap but totally manageable. You can use plastic at the bar, but people will probably look at you funny.

What you're swilling: Guinness, black and tans, Irish whiskey—you know the drill. If you're in need of an eyeopener, grab an Irish coffee.

What you're wearing: Extremely casual gear, though you'll occasionally see members of New Orleans' upper crust quaffing nightcaps in tuxedos and ball gowns

What you're hearing: The jukebox offers a wide range of tunes, but the clientele generally picks old-school rock and roll or well-worn New Orleans faves.

When you're there: Molly's is a great place to start the night. No one will get lost, yet.

Tattoo themes: Varied, depending on the crowd: sorority girls have flower anklets; bikers come with, well, biker tats. All are welcome.

Your drinking buddies: Molly's is a fiercely democratic drinking establishment. Expect to stand elbow to elbow with anyone. The joint's rotation of guest bartenders only ups the eclectic vibe. (Molly's recently let former governor and convicted felon Edwin Edwards serve drinks, if that tells you anything.)

Best feature: Molly's best feature is probably the long row of highboy tables that run from the front to the back of the room. (Picture tall picnic tables, lined with stools.) They're surprisingly comfortable, and with a little luck—or none at all—you'll walk out with a handful of new phone numbers from the group that plopped down next to you.

Everyone goes to Molly's, even when they don't know how to get there. If you tell friends from Uptown or the 'burbs to

Photograph by John d'Addario

meet you in the Quarter, Molly's is a safe bet to begin the night. Whether you start at Esplanade or Canal, if you keep walking towards the statue of Joan of Arc near the French Market, you're bound to run into Molly's.

Molly's sits on the lower part of Decatur, and though this can be the seedier end of the Quarter, this bar is too well lit and expensive to be a dive and is, in fact, a welcoming spot. The large window facing the sidewalk is always open, with patrons using the ledge as a counter for their drinks. Small tables are affixed to the balcony supports just outside the front door, allowing the party to spill out onto the sidewalk. Both act as invitations to passers-by to stop in for a drink.

We take a seat. Though certainly not Bourbon Street touristy, Molly's is *not* just a neighborhood bar. There appear to be regulars sprinkled throughout (or at least some people whom the bartender is glad to see), but then those folks join a gaggle of tourists, all of whom still proudly sport their convention nametags. Getting a bead on folks is hard here. White boys in polos sit across from heavily tattooed girls with severe, black bangs. Neither flinches.

You could come to Molly's alone, but no one really does. If you come here to get drunk, you do so with friends. Also it's a little expensive to get drunk here, unless you're doing it on beer. A dark and stormy will run you $6, though in the courtyard, it's $4.50.

Molly's is an Irish pub in that it serves Guinness, Harp, and Smithwicks and sports an Irish-themed TGI Fridays decor. Walls are crammed with signs indicating mileage to Wexford or Dublin. A faded portrait of a young Yeats hangs precariously over the bar. Trophies, photographs, and newspaper clippings are displayed haphazardly, and are those underpants nailed to the wall? Are they for sale? They look . . . worn. A six-foot poster of a rather stern Pope Pius XI looms incongruously over the bar's well-stocked jukebox. Edith Piaf and Talking Heads join the requisite Pogues, Sinatra, and Dr. John.

After half an hour, Molly's gets crowded, so we escape from the crush of the masses to the back bar in the courtyard. Though not always open, when it is, it's well worth a stop, and tonight it is less raucous than the front. There is no jukebox, and instead we listen to bartender Christine's iPod, offering a chill mix of Nina Simone and Chet Baker. Though the courtyard is covered by a Plexiglas roof, the sultry New Orleans patio vibe remains. We decide it would be really cool to sit out here in the rain and make a mental note to stop in for a drink the next time we're in the Quarter and caught in a midafternoon deluge. Drinks are cheaper out here, too, though maybe Christine was just being nice.

Name: Molly's on Toulouse
Address: 732 Toulouse Street
Phone: 504-568-1915
Your tab: Five dollars per drink
What you're swilling: Half-and-half, car bomb, whiskey
What you're wearing: A baseball cap, tank top, flip-flops
What you're hearing: Classic rock from the jukebox
When you're there: Game time; Monday–Thursday 2:00 P.M.–6:00 A.M.; Friday –Sunday 11:00 A.M.–7:00 A.M.
Tattoo themes: A mixed bag
Your drinking buddies: Locals; guys; alone is fine, too.
Best feature: No attitude

Two stools down, a young blond man sits alone and drinks a beer while watching a basketball game on the screen. "F%&★ the Knicks!" he yells. "The Knick-es. The Knick-eese." The shouting barely registers with the four guys in baseball caps at the pool table. Unlike its more crowded and touristy sister bar, Molly's at the Market, Molly's on Toulouse draws mainly locals.

The young female bartender says the blond's name, a gentle reminder that he's stepped over the line. Aside from the Tipplers, she's the only female in the place.

"F%&★," he says. "I'm drunk!" He's not angry, only surprised at how he came to this development. He shakes his head and lifts his beer glass.

French Quarter Irish Bar Mad Lib

Best bar in the Quarter! We're from (name of Northeastern city) _____ and stumbled across (name of French Quarter Irish bar) _____. (Name of female bartender) _____. took great care of us and made us feel totally at home and is kind of (sexual compliment) _____. What a relief to be away from the (expletive) _____ of Bourbon

Street. Our (name of Irish beer) _____ and (name of shot alcohol) _____were completely reasonable. See ya next time! I (verb) _____ New Orleans!

At first, it may be hard to reason why there are so many Irish bars in the Quarter. Yes, the Irish settled and reproduced in New Orleans (but where did the Irish *not* settle and reproduce?). There's also the fact that while New Orleans has been owned in turn by the by French, Spanish, French again, and American, the city has never been English—a fact that must have appealed to the Irish.

Until lately, the local Irish legacy was waning a bit. Its single remaining neighborhood event was the St. Patrick's Day parade. Uptown's Irish Channel neighborhood has long ceased to be the nexus of the working-class carpenters who, after building Garden District mansions, turned out their own modest but quaint shotgun cottages. Along with Sicilians, who saw their own local influence fade, the Irish have pretty much been relegated to an auxiliary ethnic group by New Orleans history standards. However, as if in answer to the Tipplers' query, a small museum called the Irish Cultural Museum recently opened on Conti Street. But if the Tipplers had to hazard a guess as to why there are so many Irish bars in the Quarter, the answer would have to be the simplest one of all: the Irish like to drink, and so do we.

French Quarter Irish Pub Checklist

Shamrocks!
Guinness, Harp, and Bass on tap
Surly man drinking alone
Weathered beams overhead
Bourbon Street refugee
Jägermeister shot station
Upbeat, pretty lass behind the counter

Classic-rock jukebox
Car bombs, five dollars!
Dim lighting
Funyuns

Name: Ryan's Irish Pub
Address: 241 Decatur Street
Phone: 504-523-3500
Your tab: Five dollars per drink
What you're swilling: Beer or whiskey, car bombs
What you're wearing: It's too dark to see, so no one will ever know.
What you're hearing: Classic rock and roll from the jukebox
When you're there: Anytime
Tattoo themes: Bring a flashlight and find out!
Your drinking buddies: Obscurity and a television
Best feature: Dark enough to hide anything you need to

So it's that time again: the Saints' first preseason game, a Sunday-night match against the Cardinals. The black-and-gold jerseys have been pulled out of the drawers. Throughout the city, people stop each other for impromptu sidewalk strategy sessions or simply to shout out, "Who dat?!" As we make our way towards Decatur, the windows of the bars we pass are clouded with humidity and the beery exhalations of anxious fans. Every available television in the Quarter is showing close-ups of a nervous-looking Drew Brees spitting ice cubes into his Gatorade cup on the sidelines.

Times are tough. Head coach Sean Payton has been suspended for allegedly permitting rewards for violent tackles and takedowns. New Orleanians remain divided on the point. Some are embarrassed that the underhandedness we prefer to associate with our local politicians now taints our beloved team. Others are bitter that the team is being pilloried for what they claim is a common, even if dirty, NFL practice. The familiar feeling that we've been wronged, not given our due process, has returned.

But at the moment, the even bigger question is, can the team win? They've been shaken up; the defense is sorely lacking. Our Super Bowl victory seems a distant memory. Will we be forced back into the dark days when the Saints were known as "the Aint's"? The pressure of watching proves too much for the Tipplers. We enter bars and leave without drinking. Clearly, we're not ourselves.

Finally we hit upon Ryan's, where the game isn't the only thing on television. Like many in the Quarter, Ryan's is an Irish bar. Make that a dark Irish bar. It's so dark that we can only discern the vague outlines of things—the mirror behind the bottles, the booths against the back wall. Otherwise, the corners and decor are lost to the obscurity. Since we can't see it, we ask about the draft selection and are pleased: half a dozen variations of Abita and the usual Irish suspects. Plus, the stools twist.

We opt for half-and-halfs and watch TV. Given the Saints scandal, it's been easy to forget that the rest of the country and the world has been focusing on a different sporting event. The London Olympics are in full swing; the screen over the bar shows that China and the United States are neck and neck for medals. Michael Phelps now has enough gold to buy a small continent, and a South African runner named Oscar Pistorius is making history with the sexiest-looking prosthetics known to man. Compared to the heavy emotions surrounding the Saints, the Olympics seem easy, like a feel-good date movie. We're content to pass the time watching men's gymnastics floor routines and issuing our own scores for uniforms and hairstyles. Amidst the double and triple flips, we conclude that it's time to let the somersault go as a required element.

It's easy for bars to become about other things, such as scenes or prestige or designer cocktails. From time to time, we need spots like Ryan's that are about drinking, pure and simple. We don't want a lounge or a saloon or a tavern or, God forbid, *a club*. We don't need a mixologist or even a design scheme. Ryan's reminds us of the basic reason bars began in the first place—pulling up a stool and having a pint. And while you could come here to catch up with an old friend, especially in the afternoon when you might be able to see one another, you could also come alone and not be made to feel it. You could chitchat with the young and pleasant lass behind the bar or let it be known you want to be alone and think.

CHAPTER 5

Highbrow Bars

Sometimes, you just want to dress up. Sometimes, you want to go to a nice place with clean restrooms and clean glasses to drink champagne or martinis or Sazeracs or anything else that can't be sipped from a plastic cup. This is where highbrow bars shine. They are the kind of tony places that make you want to put on a coat and tie, despite the fact that they don't usually have dress codes and that it's still 90 degrees outside.

Like L'Oréal products, highbrows cost a little more, but they're worth it. Favoring quality over quantity, these bars generally attract a mature, established clientele willing to pay for top-shelf ingredients, attentive service, and pared, considered decor. With music and flattering lighting, these are the kinds of places that make us swirl our drinks and think we've gotten somewhere in life. Their safe and elegant environs also mean that these are the kinds of bars where you can meet difficult relatives or friends of the family who take issue with New Orleans' rowdy reputation.

That's not to say that highbrow bars don't see their share of excitement. Many upscale bars take pride in creating their own simple syrups and specialty drinks with names that you won't be embarrassed to say, and sampling these original combinations can be one of the joys of high-end establishments. For those on a budget, it's worth noting that some of the bars listed here also have happy-hour specials that bring quality drinks within reach.

Name: Bar R'evolution
Address: 777 Bienville Street
Phone: 504-553-2277
Web site: www.revolutionnola.com
Your tab: High. Revolutions don't come cheap. Just ask Alexander Hamilton.
What you're swilling: Craft cocktails and nice wine
What you're wearing: Something nice, if you can. The lovely environment and drinks merit your best effort.
What you're hearing: Nice background jazz over the speaker
When you're there: Early evening is a perfect time for a predinner cocktail, or stop by later and eat in the bar.
Tattoo themes: None
Your drinking buddies: It's pretty hifalutin here.
Best feature: The Bevolo gas lanterns

New Orleans' long history can sometimes be stifling, with culture preserved as a remnant of the past. But post-Katrina, young, entrepreneurial blood has infused the city with fresh energy. This melding of modern and historic perspectives will hopefully yield a vibrant city that looks forward, with feet firmly rooted in its past. This balance is the goal of Bar R'evolution, where their drinks present the city's history with contemporary sensibilities.

Lanterns by Bevolo Gas and Electric Lights have illuminated New Orleans homes and streets for three generations. Bar R'evolution was committed to bringing that distinctive look into their bar, despite a fire code prohibiting open flames inside buildings. So they hid a special sprinkler system above each lantern inside the custom pine ceiling. That historic feel echoes throughout the bar. It is housed in a former carriageway, and its lighting, low ceiling, mercury-spotted mirror, and "liquor library" (ask the bartender) imbue this new establishment with a timeworn aura.

The cocktail menu's theme is "Louisiana's Seven Nations,"

and our orders span the globe. Elizabeth chooses the bourbon-based, Creole-influenced Presse; Allison, the Francophile, enjoys the absinthe flavor of her Henri; while Richard, a sucker for bittered liqueurs, samples the Sicilian-inspired Lorepa. All of our drinks are creative, balanced, and strong.

We admire how this bar honors New Orleans' singular character without feeling stuffy. It represents a revolution in drinking, our favorite kind.

Name: The Bombay Club
Address: 830 Conti Street
Phone: 504-586-0972
Web site: www.thebombayclub.com
Your tab: Pricey but worth it; cheaper than a trip to the West Indies
What you're swilling: Classic cocktails
What you're wearing: Something chic. The Web site notes that jackets are preferred for gentlemen, but we also saw folks in shorts.
What you're hearing: Cole Porter, Duke Ellington, and Hoagy Carmichael played on the piano
When you're there: For cocktail hour or a postdinner drink
Tattoo themes: None we can see
Your drinking buddies: Your sweetheart, your good friends
Best feature: Time travel

Enter the Bombay Club, and you step into a British men's club straight from the Ralph Lauren Colonial Collection, a perfect spot to linger after a long day of surveying your indigo plantation. The square bar anchors the room, radiating a solid, masculine presence. Its cocktail menu covers three centuries, from vintage cocktails such as the aviation and sidecar to the more modern (shudder) banana cream pie-tini. We choose a gin and tonic to keep the malaria at bay. Though the small patio behind the bar might be lovely in the spring, today is warm, so we remain inside the dim room, eschewing a seat at the bar for the cozier leather sofa adjacent to the piano.

Prince Albert gazes down, patiently and benevolently, upon the crowd, his portrait flanked by certificates noting someone's Order of Merit. Richard softly whistles "God Save the Queen," while Elizabeth and Allison suddenly feel the urge to curtsy. The piano player wraps up a Scott Joplin piece and then announces a favorite tune by Irving Berlin. All that's missing is a dog snoozing at our feet, a Lab, perhaps, to take along when we go shooting.

The cocktail hour passes, and the bar fills with dinner patrons who expect something more substantial than a pink squirrel. We intend to return one day to dine behind one of the velvet-curtained booths. Till then, we settle into the sofa, wrapped in the sounds of "You Made Me Love You," secure in our fortunes, and the guns of Verdun still far in the future.

Name: Bourbon House
Address: 144 Bourbon Street
Phone: 504-522-0111
Web site: www.bourbonhouse.com
Your tab: On the high end, but a good investment
What you're swilling: Bourbon, bourbon, and whiskey
What you're wearing: You can come in shorts, but try to make them formal.
What you're hearing: Dinner guests and a little jazz on the speaker
When you're there: Before or after dinner, though sipping on a flight midday feels decadent
Tattoo themes: None, really, though you might catch a few glimpses on the wait staff
Your drinking buddies: Whiskey fans
Best feature: 100 bourbons waiting for you to try

New Orleanians love bourbon. Residents eschewed traditional French cognac in favor of the American upstart in the early 19th century, and we've been knocking it back since, most recently at Bourbon House. Pouring almost 100 brands of American whiskies, this temple to corn liquor beckons acolytes and novices alike.

Bourbon House offers a break from the thumping music and neon of Bourbon Street, located just outside its doors. Its decor is "New Orleans-ish," and though not historic, it is tastefully executed. Dozens of golden pumpkin-shaped lanterns hang from a soaring ceiling and bathe the space in a whiskey-washed hue. The bar itself, which doubles as an oyster bar when the bivalves are in season, curves around the restaurant and easily seats 22 bourbon-loving patrons.

In the interest of research, we order the bar's bourbon flights, three small pours of related bourbons. Why have one drink when you can have three? Elizabeth chooses the Single Barrel Flight, while Allison and Richard share the Kentucky Bourbon

Distiller's Tour. Glasses are passed around, and the merits of each are mulled over. We agree the portions are generous enough that two can share a $14 flight and still get a small buzz.

Unable to declare a winner, we soon bury our noses into individual tumblers of bourbon, served on the rocks. Our visit to Bourbon House follows several nights of more down-at-the-heel venues where whiskey and soda was the default order, so this buffet of quality bourbons is a treat to our palates.

Allison passes on the straight whiskey, selecting the streetcar, a riff on the sidecar, made with bourbon and crème de cassis. The house specialty is a frozen bourbon milk punch. A bit sweet for our tastes, an extra shot of bourbon stirred in adds just enough bite.

It's worth taking two minutes to join the New Orleans Bourbon Society (N.O.B.S.). Your free membership gets you a free pour of the Bourbon of the Month, which you can sample on the spot. The card invites us to drink all of the bourbons proffered, a worthy challenge for a trio soon to finish drinking in 100 bars.

Name: Broussard's
Address: 819 Conti Street
Phone: 504-581-3866
Web site: www.broussards.com
Your tab: Moderate if you drink during happy hour
What you're swilling: Decent wine and beer selection
What you're wearing: Nothing too skimpy
What you're hearing: Jazz over the speaker
Tattoo themes: None
Your drinking buddies: Others who are in the know about this hidden gem
Best feature: The courtyard

The 18th and 19th centuries in New Orleans were smelly. Streets were covered in a sludge of human and animal waste, and most of the citizens rarely bathed. Wealthy residents, wanting to escape the stench, built courtyards behind thick walls and filled them with sweet-smelling flowers and trees. Today these architectural havens offer a different kind of refuge, where locals and visitors can dodge the noisy rabble on Bourbon Street for a spot of verdant tranquility. While many bars feature courtyards as an optional drinking location, one of the best examples of these sanctuaries is at Broussard's.

We arrive during a happy hour featuring six-dollar cocktails and wine, but we select a Paulaner Salvator and a Spaten Optimator instead. Broussard's is owned by a German family, which explains the wide German beer selection housed among the more standard Bud and Abita. Our drinks are served by Rita, a generous and friendly local who encourages us to return one day for lunch or dinner. The bar menu, featuring simple sandwiches, is available all day, while the restaurant's extensive Creole dinner menu is offered in the evenings.

Broussard's courtyard was originally part of a larger property built in 1831. The aged brick building surrounds a flagstone-paved courtyard that easily seats 70 at cast-iron tables and chairs.

Brick planters that edge the plot are filled with traditional New Orleans flora: palms, sweet olive, and crepe myrtle. One corner of the area is covered with a trellis bearing what can only be called a wisteria *tree*, since nothing about its one-foot-diameter trunk even suggests "vine." This 120-year-old flowering beauty offers a canopy from the summer sun on a hot day. Further scrutiny reveals that the wisteria is entwined with Christmas lights, which would make it lovely to sit under in the evening.

More than anything, this wisteria cements the venerable feel of the courtyard. As theme parks know, you can recreate old buildings using original brick and beams. You can even age newer materials so they blend in with the old. But you can't have 120 years of plant growth occur overnight. We linger over our beers enjoying the midday sun on this chilly October day, as so many have done before us, grateful for some peace in the historic quiet.

Name: French 75
Address: 813 Bienville Street
Phone: 504-523-5444
Web site: www.arnaudsrestaurant.com/french-75/
Your tab: High
What you're swilling: All the oldies but goodies
What you're wearing: It's too lovely in here for anything less than your best, though its proximity to Bourbon Street means the occasional T-shirt and shorts arrive.
What you're hearing: The Little Sparrow herself, Edith Piaf, over the speaker
Tattoo themes: None
Your drinking buddies: Fans of well-made drinks with cash to spare; anyone longing for Paris
Best feature: Spectacular cocktails

Some bars allow you to drink to forget, but few transport you to a better place. Arnaud's French 75 can. When we drink here, we feel rich—more specifically, rich, in Paris, in a foggy past.

The neon French 75 sign beckons to us to cross through the Bourbon Street crush and exchange its raucous clamor for Edith Piaf, who croons, *"Regardez-moi, Milord. Vous ne m'avez jamais vue. . . . "* The room hums with the contentment of people enjoying a good drink. It's our good luck to find a seat on the leopard-print loveseat stationed between the Art Deco lamps, where we wait for a bartender to arrive. There's no need to elbow our way through the rabble to order a drink tonight. French 75's table service keeps us firmly ensconced in the role of "the served." Everything here is geared to our comfort and pleasure, from the muted, flattering lighting to the majestic bar that dominates the otherwise intimate space. Though French 75 opened in 2003, the bar dates to the mid-19th century, installed here by Arnaud's when they converted a "gentleman's waiting room" into this charming, tiny saloon.

Chris Hannah pops from behind the bar to greet us, setting

down the bar's signature napkins, which bear drinking quotes from Oscar Wilde, Dorothy Parker, and our favorite from Mark Twain: "Sometimes too much to drink is barely enough." While all of the bartenders here are talented, Chris's knowledge of historic cocktails borders on encyclopedic, and if it's a slow night, be prepared to learn more than you ever imagined about the brandy crusta, widow's kiss, and, of course, French 75. There is a camp that makes the latter drink with gin in lieu of brandy. That camp is not here. If you remain skeptical, Chris has assembled a handout tracing the development of the drink and confirming brandy as its definitive spirit. We sip from our glasses, not merely barflies but well-educated connoisseurs, noting the subtle differences between the sidecar and its ancestor, the brandy crusta. We are imbued with a wealth of knowledge, a wealth. *"Non, rien de rien, non, je ne regrette rien."*

It's best to frequent French 75 when you are feeling a little impoverished. It radiates luxury, and for the price of a drink, you can bask in that warm glow. Tonight our only goal is to bask. We are well tended and well watered. Worn soles and shabby bags, obscured in the tenebrous light, are easily ignored. Meager purses somehow appear plumper. We reside in a boundless past of affluent leisure, smoothly transported there by good lighting and better booze. With sanguine smiles, we order another round. *"Quand il me prend dans ses bras, il me parle tout bas. Je vois la vie en rose."*

Name: Galvez
Address: 914 North Peters Street
Phone: 504-585-1339
Web site: www.galvezrestaurant.com
Your tab: Reasonable for the quality of the drinks
What you're swilling: Craft cocktails and good wine
What you're wearing: Something classy to match the decor
What you're hearing: Jazz standards on the speaker, endlessly
When you're there: Dusk is best, to see the river in the changing light.
Tattoo themes: None visible
Your drinking buddies: Your sweetie or someone else worth treating to the view
Best feature: The amazing view of the Mississippi River

Sometimes you go out for a drink, and instead you get a night, a dovetailing of environmental forces that create a few hours of perfection. Lee and Elizabeth visited Galvez for the view and ended up with more. . . .

Round one: Lee has been out of town for over a week, so he and I stop in Galvez to catch up over a quiet drink. The restaurant's bar provides a sweeping vista of the Mississippi River through vintage French doors that complement the exposed ceiling beams. We sit down, serenaded by a jazzy version of "Moon River," and enjoy the Mississippi now reflected in the bar's mirror.

The carafes of liquor infused with fruit and vegetables that sit along the bar and the bottle of house-made bitters all point to a craft-cocktail program. My drink is a smooth mix of pear-infused brandy, lemon, and spices, perfect for autumn. Lee sticks with his favorite, a rusty nail. We settle in to chat. When you've been with someone for several years, the familiarity is comforting and reliable but can also feel predictable and dull. Those dates when you're so excited to share who you are, and you stay out drinking and talking into the night, appear less frequently. It's hard to create that kind of magic at home, because eventually, someone is going to have to do the dishes. That's why I love visiting with Lee in a bar, where the only job is to concentrate on each other and watch the light on the Mississippi change from dusk to twilight to evening.

Round two: The music has begun to repeat, and "Moon River" rolls around again. Our bartender, Hollis Kay, grimly notes that the soundtrack, less than an hour long, haunts her nightmares. We aren't quite so bothered by the repetition and order our next libations: an old fashioned with a peach-infused bourbon for me and a Tiki drink for Lee. His punch is topped with a hollowed-out lime half into which Hollis Kay pours Chartreuse and sets on fire. We watch the flames burn. Now we're officially on a date. Discussion of domestic issues is verboten. Instead, we lean in for kisses, our knees touching.

Round three: Here's "Moon River" again. Lee says it's like the movie *Groundhog Day* and wonders when we will try to kill ourselves. Hollis Kay nods towards the river as a likely option. We both order Vieux Carré cocktails, and the dark, bitter drink complements the dark river, shimmering under the lights of the Crescent City Connection bridge. We are joking, laughing, and just a little drunk. Neither of us wants to leave.

Round four: We wisely order coffee, but I (wiser) choose the Galvez coffee, a Spanish version of my favorite after-dinner drink, café brûlot. Hollis Kay flambés a shot of brandy (more fire!) and pours that and coffee into a glass edged in sugar and cinnamon.

We sip our last drink slowly as we sit in this continuum, on a night we hope will not end, watching the endless river flow around us, the soundtrack on an endless loop, the only change our drink orders from one round to the next.

Name: Hermes Bar
Address: 725 St. Louis Street
Phone: 504-237-4144
Web site: www.antoines.com
Your tab: Happy hour is two–five dollars per drink; after that prices double.
What you're swilling: A Sazerac, a Pimm's cup, champagne
What you're wearing: Something that covers your shoulders and thighs
What you're hearing: Mostly chatter. Live swing and jazz Friday and Saturday nights.
When you're there: 4:00–7:00 P.M. (happy hour). Also, see above.
Tattoo themes: Hidden
Your drinking buddies: A healthy mix of tourists and locals
Best feature: Three-way tie among vintage krewe photographs, four-dollar glasses of champagne, and service

It's a Tuesday afternoon in the doldrums of summer and several parking miracles have just occurred, so we're in a good mood. As we sit on stools at a high table, a bow-tied server patiently explains the drink specials: four-dollar glasses of champagne and wine; two-dollar bottles of domestic beer, Abita included. He then must repeat that, as we find it hard to believe that we heard him correctly. Within moments, a cork pops in the near distance. And this can be ours every day of the week from 4:00 to 7:00 P.M. For a bar associated with Antoine's restaurant, the upscale, 1840 Creole icon next door, it seems almost too good to be true.

Like all great bars, the Hermes reveals a little of the history of the city where it resides. The bar is a shrine of sorts to the arts-centric Mardi Gras krewe of the same name and now the longest-running, night-parading krewe in New Orleans. Step up to the glass cases and you'll see a small museum's worth of photographs, scepters, and Carnival paraphernalia. In the hallway leading to the loos hangs a framed lineup of black-and-white photographs of every lily-pale queen since the krewe's inception in 1937. Each wears enough white satin and crystal beads to be seen from outer space. Suffice it to say this is a glimpse into the privileged strata of the older krewes.

With these links to our city's posh history, it's no surprise that the Hermes Bar exudes a certain feel of tradition, despite having been open only since 2009. The black-and-white mosaic floors and toasty wood paneling lend a classic, almost preppy English public school air to the place. Squint and the colored krewe flags over the mirrored bar could be the crew colors for a Thames boating club. Classic and polished, the Hermes is just upscale enough to bring out one's inner snob. We toast to a friend's acceptance into a graduate program and hear the satisfying clink of real glassware. We could also just as easily toast to our own good taste or bully on about the importance of maintaining standards. It's that kind of place, safe for parents, significant others' parents, fussy aunts, and Republicans.

But the Hermes Bar isn't so staid that you have to wonder if you belong. No one appraises your worth when you walk in. Around us are a healthy mix of tourists and locals, including a whining toddler and a suited lawyer who looks as if he just successfully settled a class action. And while you could order a mixologist-level drink, you won't impress anyone with your Johnny-come-lately knowhow. It's still connected to one of the oldest restaurants in America, so better to stay with the local favorites: a Sazerac, sidecar, or, in summer, Pimm's cup.

Perhaps it's the rows of French doors opening onto the street that keep the Hermes from feeling too cloistered. Not only do they brighten the room, but they make sure the bar doesn't lose sight of the sidewalks and the regular people who walk them. After all, though Hermes may be best known for his rather glamorous position as the athletic herald of the Greek gods, or even as a patron saint of poetry, he's also the deity of decidedly less orderly groupings: herds, weights and measures, merchants, land travel, and thieves. And with that said, happy hour is a steal (sorry).

Photograph by John d'Addario

Name: Iris
Address: 321 North Peters Street
Phone: 504-299-3944
Web site: www.irisneworleans.com
Your tab: $7.50-11 per glass of wine; $5 per beer; $10-12 per specialty cocktail, plus tip
What you're swilling: Basil-cucumber martini with St. Germain and gin. Or, for groups, the six-person punchbowl. Note: Iris has an excellent selection of single-malt scotch.
What you're wearing: Iris is elegant enough to handle whatever you put on. However, ties aren't a necessity. Think good jeans or slacks and button downs; skirts and scarves.
What you're hearing: Eclectic but tasteful and quiet—vintage country, retro swing, and big band on the speaker
When you're there: Evenings from 5:00 P.M. until close, whenever that may be. Consider a predinner drink or a nightcap. However, the reasonably priced fusion bar menu may make resisting eating difficult. Closed Sunday and Tuesday; lunch on Friday only.
Tattoo themes: Hidden from view, if there at all
Your drinking buddies: Tourists mostly; a few residents
Best feature: Local ingredients

"Considered" is a word the Tipplers often use in describing this upscale establishment. Despite a spare, box-beamed, cottagelike feel that keeps Iris from appearing too fussy or staid, make no mistake: this is a destination for refined palates and those willing to pay for top-shelf cocktails. Iris is a restaurant first but extends the same pride to its bar, especially with its fresh and locally sourced ingredients. Bitters and tonics are made by an artisan blender in a neighboring parish. Even the Van Goghesque wallpaper of the restaurant's namesake flower lining the dining room is by Flavor Paper, the high-end, design-savvy New Orleans company.

A specialty-cocktail menu includes variations on standards

such as margaritas and martinis as well as completely original, bold inventions. Whatever their origin, cocktails are crafted with care and from scratch. Patrons will see a small garden's worth of fresh herbs lining the wooden bar and, beyond, a chopping block with citrus fruits.

Once housed in the Riverbend section of Uptown, Iris has been in its North Peters location for the last couple of years. Not surprisingly, the move has meant that a greater number of Iris's patrons are now tourists. Also not surprisingly, the majority of its clientele are mature professionals. A significant number are also guests at the adjoining and similarly understated Bienville Hotel.

And when the weather cooperates, Iris has another ace in its pocket: those ordering drinks can take them outside and sip in the hotel's tasteful courtyard just beyond the bar. Complete with a saltwater pool, this diminutive oasis is a detail that the Tipplers are tucking away for next summer.

Name: Mr. B's Bistro
Address: 201 Royal Street (at Iberville Street)
Phone: 504-523-2078
Web site: www.MrBsBistro.com
Your tab: You're at a bar in the middle of one of New Orleans' better restaurants. You're not going to be drinking PBR. Break out the credit card and go to town.
What you're swilling: Order up a glass of wine or a martini, or challenge the bartenders with a long-forgotten cocktail. Not that you'll stump them, but hey, you can try.
What you're wearing: There's no dress code, but you'll feel more comfortable in something a little dressy: proper trousers, collared shirts, cocktail dresses—you get the picture. In a pinch, you can whip out the khakis and a Hawaiian shirt, but we may not sit near you.
What you're hearing: The murmur of conversation and the sound of plates on marble-topped tables
Tattoo themes: Is "discreet" a theme?
Your drinking buddies: During the day, you're likely to find quite a few locals, since Mr. B's is a popular place for business lunches. At night, the pendulum swings towards tourists, but not the Bourbon Street type (well, not usually).
Best feature: The decor is stunning—probably the most "bistro" of all the bistros in town.

We don't often run ahead of schedule, but tonight, it's happened. We're on our way to meet friends at Green Goddess, one of the best restaurants in the Quarter but also one of the smallest. There's no bar there, and no real waiting area, so rather than show up ahead of our group and stand around twiddling our thumbs, we've decided to slow our roll and stop at Mr. B's for a quick drink.

It's one of the best ideas we've had in a long time—and one of the worst.

"Best" because Mr. B's is a great restaurant: elegant but not stuffy, beautiful but not prissy. Also, the drinks are exceptional, and the bartenders world-class pros.

"Worst" because we're starving, and the food at Mr. B's smells amazing. Halfway through our cocktails, Richard asks the hostess if we could maybe kind of, you know, slide into one of the few nearby open tables for a quick snack, pretty please?

Two minutes later, we've ordered five appetizers for three people—though in fairness, two of those are garlic-truffle fries because, c'mon, garlic . . . truffle . . . fries? If there are three words in the English language that ought to be permanently linked to one another, it's those.

Thirty minutes later, we waddle out, wondering how on earth we'll make it through another meal. But we manage.

Name: Orleans Grapevine Wine Bar and Bistro
Address: 720 Orleans Street
Phone: 504-523-1930
Web site: www.orleansgrapevine.com
Your tab: A bit high; purchasing a bottle gets you a better deal
What you're swilling: Good wine, though they have a full bar if the grape isn't your thing
What you're wearing: Varies from tourist fare to suits
What you're hearing: Anything from U2 to Stevie Wonder on the player piano
When you're there: In the evening
Tattoo themes: None
Your drinking buddies: Folks who aren't interested in hand grenades or three-for-one anything
Best feature: The charming courtyard, a real gem

Drinking in the French Quarter brings visions of either abundance (hurricanes, hand grenades, and big ass beers) or tradition (Sazeracs and Pimm's cups). A quality pinot noir or an oaky chardonnay aren't the usual bill of fare. But if wine is your tipple of choice, there is one spot in the Quarter that beckons with class.

The Grapevine sits on Orleans Street, just behind St. Louis Cathedral. Elizabeth has just finished work and is a bit peckish, so our friends Anthony and Lester suggest the Grapevine, which offers a varied late-night menu and the ambiance of an Italian *enoteca*. We perch on some of the 12 seats around the granite, U-shaped bar near the wrought-iron cabinet that houses the bar's red wine. We ask our adorable bartender, Korey, for wine recommendations from their extensive wine list, and soon we are sharing a lovely pinot noir and nibbling on crab cakes from their small-plates menu. Anthony notes that the kitchen serves until midnight on weekends, worth remembering if you are hungry and don't want standard bar fare.

Anthony insists we visit the courtyard, so we take our bottle

Photograph by John d'Addario

to finish outside. The high walls, fountain, and tall banana plants create a landscaped charm, more considered than many bar courtyards around the Quarter. Heaters keep the courtyard cozy in early December, so we are warmed by the lamps as well as the wine. It's hard to believe we are half a block from Bourbon Street, immured from the noise and rabble. We lean back in our chairs and admire the stars, not a speck of neon in sight.

Photograph by John d'Addario

Name: Patrick's Bar Vin
Address: 730 Bienville Street (in the St. Louis Hotel)
Phone: 504-200-3180
Web site: www.patricksbarvin.com
Your tab: $12 per drink, including tip
What you're swilling: Pinot noir or a house-specialty cocktail
What you're wearing: A little black dress; a button down and loafers
What you're hearing: Midcentury jazz on the speaker
When you're there: For a predinner cocktail or a nightcap
Tattoo themes: Well covered, if there at all
Your drinking buddies: Husbands and wives, second husbands and wives, business colleagues, people who own wine fridges
Best feature: Wine selection

Despite the fact that less than half a block separates Bar Vin from the mayhem and splatter of Bourbon Street, this European wine bar—discreet, upscale, and quiet—feels a hemisphere away. The Tipplers step past the wall and iron gate lining Bienville, and suddenly hooting tourists, Journey cover songs, and daiquiri cups disappear.

Instead, the Tipplers are greeted by a bubbling fountain, a small brick patio, and bistro tables. It's the kind of tiny and delightful secret the Quarter is fond of keeping. These handkerchief-sized peek-a-boo courtyards are the architectural equivalent of lingerie. And even if this little oasis can't cool New Orleans in late July (even at full throttle, our air conditioners barely can), it feels better here.

We step farther in, past a narrow salon, and are greeted by a sophisticated, decidedly upscale space that evokes a gentlemen's club (think London, not Bourbon Street). Paneled walls; leased wine lockers, each with an engraved nameplate of its current patron; and upholstered, Napoleonic era-inspired chairs speak of privilege. Eight leather stools line a slender but well-stocked bar, while three sets of French doors span the wall opposite. Just beyond these waits the large center atrium, a space shared with the St. Louis Hotel, where Patrick's is housed.

Run by an affable, Belgian-born oenophile, Patrick's features an extensive wine list, both by the glass and the bottle, that demonstrates a commitment to quality. But the bar also offers an inventive, recherché list of specialty cocktails, including ingredients the Tipplers especially favor, such as bourbon, St. Germain, champagne, and fresh oranges, lemons, and grapefruits. Given the heat outside, we opt for the gently iced.

Because ingredients are squeezed and measured, shaken and strained, it can take a good fifteen minutes to get a round at Patrick's. But we all agree the cocktails are worth the wait and the price. Perhaps in an effort at noblesse oblige or simply to pull in more locals, Patrick's does offer five-dollar specials—French wines by the glass on Tuesday and Thursday—a bargain by Quarter standards.

It's not surprising that the crowd is spare and mature, coiffed and cigarette free. Most likely they are guests at the hotel, repeat customers from last night. Tastefully tipsy and content to be just a little naughty, they keep holding out their oversized wineglasses and calling out, "Patrick! Patrick!" Ever the genial host, and usually onsite, Patrick Van Hoorebeek is willing to oblige and offer insight into the wine menu. Each Tippler registers the moment and tucks away Patrick's for the evening we know is inevitable—the visit from a discriminating relative.

But on this sultry July evening, it's all about us, and the Tipplers opt to take their cocktails to the atrium, a rare spread of climate-controlled, mosquito-free, nearly outside space. And it's here that we sit and sip and, despite 88 bars to go, are in no hurry to leave.

Name: The Rib Room Bar
Address: 621 St. Louis Street (in the Omni Royal Orleans)
Phone: 504-529-7045
Web site: www.ribroomneworleans.com
Your tab: $5 for a beer, $10 for a specialty cocktail
What you're swilling: Sidecars, French 75s (with gin), old fashioneds, mojitos, margaritas
What you're wearing: Corporate casual; cocktail attire
What you're hearing: Piano jazz and lounge standards
When you're there: Friday and Saturday night, Sunday after mass
Tattoo themes: None
Your drinking buddies: Hotel guests, post-cathedral Sunday crowd, families
Best feature: Self-assurance

In ages when famine was often only one bad harvest away, the tables of royalty groaned with joints of meat. If you had meat, you had money. This message has survived through the centuries, perhaps most visibly in the form of steakhouses. Inevitably, certain strata are drawn to these locales: the captains of industry and the titans of finance. These are people known as "makers" in the lingo of the most recent presidential election.

Steakhouses are generally class-controlled environments. Temples to red meat, they often share a common decor: dark paneling, leather, and tapestries. Interestingly, these spaces are usually windowless—perhaps to focus all attention on the privilege within or to prevent the rabble from pressing their grubby noses to the glass and peering in. Reliably groomed and professional servers are easily identifiable by uniforms and nametags.

The Rib Room Bar shares many of these exclusive qualities. Occupying a middle space between the restaurant proper and the lobby corridor, the bar offers table service at highboys or a seat at the granite bar itself, with its almost cosmically glowing shelves and a trompe l'oeil blue-sky dome that may replace the need to see the real thing. The bar's dramatic decor is highlighted by 18-foot ceilings and an 8-foot gilt mirror that adorns the back wall. A single, discreet television above the bar is a nod to the crowds who come here to watch LSU and Saints games while enjoying a $10 top-shelf bloody mary.

However, for those interested in the world outside its hallowed walls, the Rib Room Bar does offer spectacular views of the Beaux Arts Supreme Court Building across St. Louis Street in one direction and the charm of Royal Street in the other. Because the bar is in a large hotel, it offers the kind of proportions that most bars in the Quarter can't.

Also keeping the Rib Room Bar from being just an extension of a typical steakhouse is the fact that, on weekends, a talented singer performs a standard lounge playlist. Tonight she croons "'S Wonderful" without a trace of irony. It's not the kind of wild jazz and blaring horns that New Orleans is known for, but it is safe and accessible and inspires several of the more mature couples to rise from their stools and take a twirl across the carpet.

CHAPTER 6

Dive Bars

There's a reason dive bars are called dives; here's where you can lower your standards and let yourself sink, round by round, until gravity has its way. Here you don't have to sit up straight or offer witticisms or profound insights. Here your vocabulary suddenly becomes centered on words you'd never say in church. And cheap drinks mean that it's easier to ignore the inner voice that says it's probably time to go home. At some point, you become aware that you are a hangover in the making and then make a final, conscious decision not to care. In dives, you can also expect brands of vodka and whiskey you've never heard of to fill the well. You can also expect a plastic cup and hose-friendly floors.

In many ways, dive bars are close relatives of neighborhood bars, and in some cases, such as the Abbey, that's how they started out. The difference is that neighborhood bars feel chummy and upbeat—places for great conversation. Dive bars aren't about conversations, at least not intelligible ones. Dive bars are about getting completely, irrevocably hammered and exorcizing the woes of the world. In them, you can feel gritty and rough and like it.

However, what's interesting about New Orleans' dive bars—especially those in the French Quarter—is that they don't discriminate. Look up from your shot glass, and you might find yourself in the midst of a wedding party or a group of gala-goers who've gone slumming after the symphony. Or you could find yourself surrounded by drunks and junkies. For better or worse, dive bars are like mini anthropological excursions.

So for the price of a draft beer, take a stool in a dive and settle in to witness life's rich pageant.

Name: The Abbey
Address: 1123 Decatur Street
Phone: 504-523-7177
Your tab: So very, very cheap
What you're swilling: Beer, a shot, beer and a shot
What you're wearing: Dirty black; Eye Hate God T-shirt; a wallet with a chain
What you're hearing: Punk and gutter punk on the jukebox
When you're there: Better to end here than to start the night
Tattoo themes: Dark, possibly angry, and possibly on your face and neck
Your drinking buddies: Fellow gutter punks and Quarter Rats
Best feature: The ladies' room

We enter the Abbey and laugh. Allison is in yellow, Elizabeth is in sherbet, and everyone else in the bar (including Richard) is in black. But despite this sartorial dissonance, no one bats an eye at the springy attire. The Abbey (which locals affectionately call "the Scabby") may be a dive, but it's the best kind of dive, where anyone is welcome.

The Abbey sits on the edge of lower Decatur, once Gallatin Street, a 19th-century den of inequity, home to ne'er-do-wells and denizens of the wharves. That seedy vibe remains. The setting is punk cathedral, and grimy, stained-glass windows on the wall and above the bar make the Abbey a kind of temple to drinking. Though the clientele can range from off-duty stripper to off-duty cop, tonight it houses a gaggle of gutter punks so grubby that their black clothes look dirty.

Unfortunately, their slovenly aesthetic extends to their bathing habits, and soon the Tipplers are awash in the inescapable aroma of B.O. But in the name of research we persevere, finding seats and ordering a well-poured well whiskey for $3.50 and two pints of High-Life for a mere $2 each. There's nothing to lure the average tourist here: no drink specials, hurricanes, or frozen concoctions. We imagine that the dim lighting leaves them wondering if it's even open, and for those who might pop their heads in, the smell discourages patronage. There's certainly no one here who wasn't already planning to come here. The Abbey is not merely local, but it feels like the kind of bar where everyone knows each other, or at least they do tonight.

The tight camaraderie emerges as patrons belt out a rousing chorus of "F%&★ You, I'm Drunk," to which there is much swaying and sloshing of PBR and whiskey. This demonstration nudges the Tipplers to the jukebox, where X and the Dead Kennedys are joined by several CDs with handwritten labels listing songs by the Mentors and Agent Orange. Though the *mise en scène* of the Abbey is grunge dishabille, one area remains an unsullied oasis: the ladies' bathroom. It is the best-lit room in the bar and is embellished with a mural depicting a scene straight out of *The Sound of Music*. Part of its beauty is its unexpectedness, but even regular patrons appreciate its attributes. When Allison visits the ladies' room, both women and men are waiting to use it. This is not a case of transgendered bathroom usage. Instead, the very straight looking guy behind her prefers the nicer women's loo over the dirty men's. Apparently, even the unwashed like to pee somewhere pretty.

We don't linger after our first round, though our wallets nudge us to do so. Tonight the Abbey is for regulars, not the odd visitor. We head for a more comfortable and more aromatic locale, with a vision of the Alps still fresh in our minds.

Photograph by John d'Addario

Name: The Alibi
Address: 811 Iberville Street
Phone: 504-522-9187
Web site: www.alibineworleans.com
Your tab: Depends on whether you're ordering, Bud or Chimay
What you're swilling: Good beer and post-shift shots
What you're wearing: What you went to work in
What you're hearing: The game on the TV, whatever's on the iPod
When you're there: After your shift
Tattoo themes: All are welcome.
Your drinking buddies: Service-industry comrades
Best feature: Your drinking buddies

In most of America, the five-o'clock whistle blows and people pause for an after-work drink. But folks who leave work when most of America is in bed deserve a place to unwind too. Waiters, hostesses, line cooks, sous chefs, bartenders, bouncers, and even strippers all warrant a convivial spot with happy-hour prices, even at midnight. Enter the Alibi.

Located on Iberville near Bourbon, the Alibi is close enough to that great soggy thoroughfare to get some tourist traffic, but its lack of flash means most tourists pass it by. After 11:00 P.M., though, it is a service-industry hub, and the bar is a sea of waiters in oxford-cloth shirts. Though some might call the Alibi a dive, its varied beer selection speaks to clientele with higher-end tastes. Chimay, Unibroue, Spaten, and Harp nestle alongside Bud and Coors. The chatter focuses on the previous shift; lousy tippers and demanding patrons are skewered. Job openings are explored. Eavesdropping here gives one behind-the-scenes insight you'll never find in Zagat. As the clientele becomes more lubricated, the topics shift to more mundane affairs: the Saints, rising rents, the merits of one veterinarian versus another. Troubles are sloughed off and optimism settles in. Patrons lean in, perhaps to hear themselves above the growing din, or merely to cozy up to that cute new server from the Palace Café. We see one waiter give her colleague a frank visual appraisal before scooting in closer; in their matching shirts, they look like a couple who just abandoned a Sadie Hawkins dance.

While the Alibi offers food of the bar/fried variety, some folks settle their tabs and head out for more varied fare. But others feel that 1:00 A.M. is drinking time, not dinnertime, regardless of when they left work. They order another round, moving full circle from server to served. The happy hour has worked its magic.

Name: Aunt Tiki's
Address: 1207 Decatur Street
Phone: 504-680-8454
Your tab: Cheap
What you're swilling: The basics: bourbon and Coke, vodka and soda, beer. (In fact, the beer selection isn't half-bad.) If someone had a lucky night at the casino, you may encounter a round of complimentary shots with embarrassingly lurid names.
What you're wearing: Anything casual—in fact, the more casual, the better. Shirts with collars are almost a no-no.
What you're hearing: The jukebox is pretty damn good. You're just as likely to hear '80s new wave as thrash metal.
When you're there: Anytime, day or night—although more genteel types might want to stick to premidnight quaffing. The locals get rowdy later on.
Tattoo themes: Old-school mermaids, full sleeves, and the occasional homemade prison tat
Your drinking buddies: Locals—some from the service industry, some gainfully unemployed, and some just from the neighborhood. All are friendly (though you know how some folks can get testy when they drink).
Best feature: Dim lighting. Very dim, like Steak-and-Ale-circa-1984 dim. If there's one thing that doesn't mix well with booze, it's light, and Aunt Tiki's knows it.

Ages ago, Aunt Tiki's was a gay bar—an awesome, raunchy gay bar, with a bathtub stashed in a back room. (It was not used for bathing, per se.) Now, Aunt Tiki's is mostly straight and neighborhood-ish, but on some nights, the joint returns to its jubilant, raucous roots, with locals reveling in one another's daily triumphs. Someone just got a job: shots for everybody! Someone's moving tomorrow: another round of Jägermeister! At those times, the energy is infectious, and it spills out the front door onto Decatur Street, taking the crowd with it.

But tonight, Aunt Tiki's is its other self: a drinkers' bar. Folks are still friendly, and you see a couple of young patrons cutting up in the corner, but generally speaking, things are quiet. The bartender brings our drinks—a Budweiser, an Abita, and a rum and Coke—and smiles, but she's not going to engage in conversation. She wanders over to the jukebox, pops in a couple of bucks, and picks out some indie-rock options and a punk tune or two. It doesn't change the mood, just gives it a slightly different soundtrack. At the end of a long night spent at much louder bars, that's about all we want.

Name: The Bar at Congo Square
Address: 718 North Rampart Street (at Orleans Street)
Phone: 504-265-0953
Your tab: Cheap
What you're swilling: Beer, bourbon, Baileys—take your pick. Just please, not all three. At least not at once.
What you're wearing: Anything more than a thong and a tank top is fine, unless it's Carnival, in which case you can probably leave the tank top at home.
What you're hearing: It varies, but recently, the bar has been home to some late-night parties featuring very good dance ditties on the speaker.
Tattoo themes: None to speak of, but nevertheless, the ink is abundant. Given the low-key, homey nature of the joint, though—and the clientele—tats aren't usually extravagant. Expect to see names, fleurs-de-lis, cartoon characters, and other flash impulsively picked off the walls at neighborhood tattoo parlors.
Your drinking buddies: This is a local hangout, drawing a mostly LGBT crowd from the Quarter and surrounding neighborhoods. Tourists are welcome, but given the bar's slightly out of the way location, there aren't many on hand.
Best feature: Its utter lack of pretense. If you're looking for a comfy place to plop down and toss 'em back, you've found it.

It's 1:00 A.M. when Richard turns to Elizabeth and asks, "How the hell did we get here?" It's a common refrain.

Like the Ninth Circle a few doors down, Congo Square is a late-night bar. In most places it would be called an "after-hours bar," but since our bars don't close, "after-hours" is a foreign concept to New Orleanians, like instant coffee or snow. And yet, it's not completely depraved in here. There's a party going on in the back, with music and dancing and 20somethings cutting up, but out front where we are, folks from the neighborhood sit and gossip while quaffing a few gin and tonics.

It's that kind of duality that makes Congo Square the perfect place to end the evening—or start it.

Without warning, three of our friends come dancing out of the back and drag us into the mix. They've caught us at the perfect time: tipsy enough to get down but sober enough to get back up again. Half an hour later, we emerge, happy and exhausted and sweaty and ready for bed, or maybe one more shot.

Name: Coop's Place
Address: 1109 Decatur Street
Phone: 504-525-9053
Web site: www.CoopsPlace.net
Your tab: Totally reasonable—but then again, this isn't the place to get all fancy with your libations. In fact, don't call them "libations" while you're here, okay?
What you're swilling: Take your pick, but if you ask us, don't miss out on Coop's good selection of beer.
What you're wearing: A T-shirt and jeans; or perhaps a T-shirt and shorts; or if you prefer, a T-shirt and a skirt. If it requires dry-cleaning, leave it at the hotel.
What you're hearing: Whatever's on the jukebox. Chances are good that it'll be hipstery rock, though.
Tattoo themes: This is lower Decatur Street. If you want to impress people with your tats, they ought to be stellar, designed and inked by Belgian artists who only visit the U.S. for three hours during the full moon every other leap year. Cover up the Tweety Bird and the Tasmanian Devil, for your own safety.
Your drinking buddies: Coop's Place is loosely divided into a restaurant and bar. The restaurant tends to attract a mix of locals and tourists, with slightly more emphasis on the latter. The bar, on the other hand, is straight-up Quarter Rat.
Best feature: The food. If you're making a night of it—and if you're at Coop's, you probably are—you need some nourishment to blunt your buzz. Coop's may look divey, but its menu is fantastic. In fact, it's one of the few places in Orleans Parish where you can find good Cajun food (not Creole, and not soul food). Try the boudin. It's a life-changer.

We didn't plan to come to Coop's tonight—really, we didn't. We were on our way to a party around the corner when the sky suddenly opened up and the rain poured down. Like a port in a storm, Coop's was there.

Nighttime showers are unusual here, so there's no telling how long we'll be marooned on this boozy island. We decide to make the most of it with a few rounds of beer.

An hour later, the rain is still coming down hard. If we were so inclined, we could make a run for the party, but the idea of arriving soaked to the skin in a room full of strangers isn't all that attractive. The host is really just a friend of a friend—an acquaintance at best. To be honest, we were mostly going to see her apartment, which is legendary. Also, she lives near a couple of Hollywood A-listers, and as jaded as we try to be, we have kind of a soft spot for celebs—some of them, anyway.

We look towards the front door, wondering if it'll ever let up.

"Tropical storm," says the guy to our right, matter-of-factly. He looks as if he lives here—and by "here" we mean "at the bar." He digs around in his pocket. "Popped up last night. On its way toward Alabama." He pulls out a cell phone and shows us the storm track, proving his point.

Oh well, that's more reason for us to stay parked right where we are and down a few more drinks, and a couple of bowls of jambalaya, and oh, maybe some of that boudin. After another 30 minutes, the bartender passes out shots. We don't know what they are, and we don't ask. As we lift the glasses to our lips, our new friend offers a toast: "To hunkering down and drinking up." Even if he doesn't live here, he talks like a local.

Name: Copper Monkey
Address: 725 Conti Street
Phone: 504-527-0869
Your tab: Five to six dollars per drink, including tip
What you're swilling: Southern Hops'pitality IPA by Lazy Magnolia on draft
What you're wearing: Company polo shirt, T-shirt
What you're hearing: Classic rock and roll on the speaker
When you're there: Before or after something else, football games
Tattoo themes: Varied
Your drinking buddies: Service-industry folk, tourists
Best feature: Small but quality regional-draft selection

It's Saturday night, and the Tipplers stop into the Copper Monkey for a quick round before heading out to a late show at One Eyed Jacks. The Copper Monkey is that kind of bar. Unless you're there to settle in for a game and grub (standard bar fare), the Monkey probably isn't your destination. Instead, it's a refueling station, a warm-up for or wind-down from the main event.

Or like the groomed, middle-aged couple wearing Ole Miss beads and leaning into each other for support, the Monkey might be the place where you realize you peaked early and now need to call it quits. But it's exactly that undefined, transitory nature of the Quarter that lures the Tipplers back time after time. With everything so close and everyone on foot, the Quarter doesn't ask for commitments. Any place can be a possibility, even if only for 15 minutes.

Though unexceptional, the Copper Monkey, to its credit, doesn't try to be anything else. Aside from the bar, which dominates the room, a row of small tables flanks one wall and a kitchen occupies the back. Somehow it manages to find space for six televisions, all currently broadcasting college games; a football pool has been taped to the mirror by the register. You can order hurricanes and bloody marys from buckets with stoppers or, like the two flushed-faced chefs in their black and whites, a bucket of Budweisers. The Copper Monkey does have a small, quality selection of regional brews such as Canebrake and Lazy Magnolia on tap.

If this stretch of Conti were more residential, the Copper Monkey would certainly be considered a neighborhood bar. As it is, the locals are likely to be service-industry folk getting off shifts or on furtive breaks, like the cooks chain smoking American Spirits across the bar or the server who shares some gossip with the on-duty bartender and then sits next to us for a quick round. Like us, they'll all be gone in a few minutes, moving on to other places.

Name: Deja Vu Bar and Grill
Address: 400 Dauphine Street
Phone: 504-523-1931
Web site: www.dejavunola.com
Your tab: Low
What you're swilling: Beer, strong booze and mixers, good bloody marys
What you're wearing: It's pretty casual in here, though if you stop in late after a fancy shindig in evening wear, no one will look at you funny.
What you're hearing: Classic rock on the speaker
When you're there: Into the night; post-drinking for late-night/early-morning food
Tattoo themes: We see all kinds, including several full sleeves.
Your drinking buddies: Lots of locals who know a good deal when they see one
Best feature: Good food and drinks at great prices

Gastro pubs are cropping up around the country. Since they are part bar and part restaurant, you go there to get one thing and end up staying for the other. Deja Vu figured out long ago that when you serve food and booze 24/7, no one leaves. Though Deja Vu offers neither the bar menu nor the specialty cocktails of its contemporaries, its fare will keep your belly and spirit happy, and on the cheap at that.

Most patrons in the dim, smoky room are eating, which might lead you to think Deja Vu functions primarily as a restaurant. But the smoke should also be a clue to its true status. Smoking remains permitted in bars here, not restaurants, so the gentleman happily chasing cancer on his barstool confirms that we are in a saloon. The decor also leans towards "bar," with a heavy presence of Miller High Life and Regal beer signs from the 1960s. The claw and video-poker machines seal the aesthetic deal.

We sit at the bar and order the basics: beer, whiskey and soda, a shot. It's best to stick with the standards, though Elizabeth sampled a very decent bloody mary here one recent morning, along with some hangover eggs. The aroma of food nudges us to order our favorite appetizer, the fried green beans. Richard reminisces about his days of youth, working around the corner at Lucky Cheng's, an Asian-themed, drag-queen-staffed restaurant (now, sadly closed). The staff there often ordered from Deja Vu, and Richard remembers that the food was both tasty and delivered on time, *even on Mardi Gras Day*. The Lucky Cheng's staff also frequently stopped here for cheap, post-shift drinks.

Deja Vu's hours accommodate folks from the service industry, so even though tourists fill some of the tables, it still reads local. The bartender greets patrons, and patrons greet each other in a convivial and familiar atmosphere.

Is it a restaurant? Is it a bar? No matter the hour, somehow it always manages to be both, equally well.

Name: The Dungeon
Address: 738 Toulouse Street
Phone: 504-523-5530
Your tab: If you stick with beer and the standards, you do okay. Tabs go up when you start ordering their specialty drinks.
What you're swilling: They have a pretty well stocked bar, but you'll get a funny look if you order a rusty nail or sidecar.
What you're wearing: Break out the studded collar and the chaps if you've got them. Leather accessories also make appearances. An old NIN or Pantera T-shirt will do too.
What you're hearing: Lots of metal from various decades on the speaker
Tattoo themes: Given the theme of the bar, all ink is welcome and in abundance.
Your drinking buddies: Metalheads, Goth kids, curious tourists
Best feature: Cage booths

When you visit a bar called the Dungeon, you enter with expectations of a dim, prisonlike space filled with cells or cages and maybe some torture devices. The Dungeon supplies all of that, in spades. We drop in the weekend before Halloween, hoping to witness illicit acts but willing to settle for anything more interesting than the typical Slutty Nurse lurching down Bourbon Street.

The entrance through a narrow door leads us down a long alley to a small courtyard in front of the actual bar. As the Dungeon is located just off Bourbon Street, this walk serves as a transition from one kind of debauchery to another, the latter a little darker and naughtier than the three-for-one, neon aesthetic half a block away. Gavin came here in the early '90s on a road trip from San Francisco and notes that not much has changed. Though we are at street level, the low ceiling makes us feel as though we are heading underground. The decor inside is grimy S&M meets the Haunted Mansion. Some vaguely racy bondage lithographs hang on the walls next to a medieval-looking crossbow. Signs warn that video is strictly forbidden, but truthfully, there isn't much to record. Instead, some rather conventionally clad patrons are drinking and dancing to a mix of Def Leppard, Depeche Mode, and Uriah Heep. Indeed it's the bartenders who sport the most interesting attire, somewhere just shy of '80s punk with big neon hair, ripped leggings, and numerous bangles. We think it might not be a costume.

What would normally be booths are benches set in cages, and we snag a cage installed at the end of the bar. The size of a ski-lift gondola, it encloses us, and quartered in our pen we enjoy an incongruous intimacy in the midst of the blaring Pantera. It's clear that we have scored the best cage in the bar. Its location allows our bartender to easily check on us, a convenience that reminds Elizabeth of a swim-up bar. Here, too, we never have to leave our party to get a drink.

Later in the night we drink in the upstairs bar, which is covered in skulls and features a wall with four manacles attached, presumably to shackle and whip eager masochists. There are no takers tonight and we wonder if it's only in use on certain nights, the way other bars reserve evenings for dart or billiard clubs.

New Orleans offers a promise of forbidden fruit to folks who live mostly vanilla lives. While the Dungeon is not the underground den of iniquity that it used to be, it still holds its own as a place where metalheads can shake their manes and leather fans can brandish their crops with enthusiasm.

Name: Gold Mine Saloon
Address: 701 Dauphine Street
Phone: 504-586-0745
Web site: www.goldminesaloon.net
Your tab: Three-dollar cover, plus your drinks
What you're swilling: Flaming Dr. Pepper shots
What you're wearing: Tasteful flirt wear
What you're hearing: Beyonce, Lady Gaga on the speaker
When you're there: After midnight Friday and Saturday; closed Monday and Tuesday
Tattoo themes: Greek letters
Your drinking buddies: The undergraduates of Tulane and Loyola universities
Best feature: Dancing

"It's 11 now. Wait an hour and you'll see this place turn," says the Tipplers' guide for this Saturday evening. Our friend, a self-described "frequent Gold Mine offender," has organized this outing to show us his former favorite haunt. He's timed our visit to avoid the Gold Mine's peak, allowing us plenty of time before its descent into what he calls "the dark hours." It's clear that he speaks from firsthand knowledge. In the meantime, he and the Tipplers warm up the dance floor while a DJ spins overhead from his plastic-walled roost—contemporary dance mixes tilted heavily towards hip-hop and pop.

The Gold Mine is a dive by anyone's standards, a largish cave of black walls, cement floors, and brick arches à la Poe's "The Cask of Amontillado." An entire corner is devoted to '80s iconic video games—PacMan, Frogger, Defender, Space Invaders, all now sadly defunct. Likewise, the Gold Mine appeals to those who are now between the ages of fake ID and 25. Elizabeth, who grew up across Lake Pontchartrain, realizes that it's her first time back to the Gold Mine since high school, when the drinking age in Louisiana was something like 14. That said, the Gold Mine is too casual to be a scene and so without attitude that anyone is welcome. And the Tipplers do get a small thrill from being *carded*.

The only draft beer is unidentified and tastes a little less strong than Coors. There's a spinning wheel with drink names on it, but it always seems to come up on the favorite—flaming Dr. Pepper shots. So while we wait for midnight, we order a round. The bartenders work in tandem, lining up the beer glasses, adding an amaretto-like substance, and flicking their Bics. Somehow the foaming concoction manages to taste exactly like Dr. Pepper. It's the kind of resourcefulness that keeps America a world leader.

Sure enough, at midnight, small bands of young men and women begin passing through the turnstiles. Some of them don't even head to the bar and simply erupt in spontaneous dance. There's an almost innocent Annette Funicello/Frankie Avalon quality to the way they rush into the songs. Judging by the chic mini dresses, highlighted long hair, Ralph Lauren shirts, and our guide's own experience, most of the Gold Mine's patrons are Tulane or Loyola students or recent grads who are now among the young-professional ranks. For the Quarter, the crowd is extremely white and privileged.

We watch our ambassador for the evening attempt to maneuver his loafers towards a young lady whose orange shirt glows preternaturally under the white lights. She proves a difficult catch, and though the Tipplers stay a while, no results are forthcoming. Our guide remains undeterred. He's a veteran miner and knows there's plenty of time before the dark hours of desperate and questionable judgments set in. Our own curfew, however, has passed. We wave goodbye and hope he strikes gold.

Name: Jimani
Address: 141 Chartres Street
Phone: 504-524-0493
Your tab: Cheapo!
What you're swilling: Beer specials and strong booze with a mixer are recommended.
What you're wearing: Post-shift clothes
What you're hearing: Rock and roll, old and new, played on the speaker *really loud*
When you're there: Late at night, tackling your munchies
Tattoo themes: *Allll* themes
Your drinking buddies: Whoever else is hungry, thirsty, and broke
Best feature: Cheap, cheap drinks!

Jimani offers more than you need of everything. Ten TVs cover most of the available wall space, while the rest is obscured by hundreds, possibly thousands, of photos of patrons through the years. The driving theme behind their (almost) 24-hour menu is "more": more sausage, more bacon, more cheese, all featured in the Hang Ova Burger, Jimmy J's Big Ass Nachos, and the House Garbage Salad. The music is also more, and talking with your party requires shouting above the din.

Jimani's drink specials include five High Lifes or PBRs for $10. You can probably find similar deals in other divey bars around the Quarter, but Jimani holds its own, pouring some of the strongest, cheapest drinks in the Vieux Carré. Even in the dim light, Elizabeth's $3.75 whiskey and soda is pure gold, not the pale yellow served in most bars.

This isn't a place for a quiet conversation, but if you are hungry and want a lively spot to watch whatever sporting event floats your boat while sipping on some of the best-priced drinks in the Quarter, Jimani is your place.

Name: Last Call
Address: 806 Conti Street
Phone: 504-529-1833
Your tab: Five to seven dollars per drink
What you're swilling: A bottle of beer and a well shot (see below)
What you're wearing: Flip-flops, shorts, and a tank top, either for a man or woman
What you're hearing: Decent rock and roll or vintage R&B on the jukebox
When you're there: Dinner to sunrise
Tattoo themes: Fleurs-de-lis and axes
Your drinking buddies: Tourists, Bourbon Street musicians, service-industry folk
Best feature: The $10 Chef Paul's House of Wings plate (Cajun buffalo sauce)

It's not last call, not even second-to-last call. In fact, it's 6:00 P.M. on a Thursday. So since it seems unlikely that we two Tipplers will last another 12 hours, we ask the bartender if there is, in fact, a last call. He admits that on some nights there isn't.

"So this is a little weird, but your receipt," he tells Allison, "will say chicken tender. And yours," he points to Elizabeth, "will say extra tender."

None of us has ordered chicken tenders. Instead, what we've asked for is the Last Call's eternal special: five dollars for a "cheap" beer and a shot from the well, and seven dollars for an "expensive" beer and a shot of anything except top shelf.

Elizabeth beams at her receipt. "I always knew I was extra tender."

Allison shakes her head. "I always knew I wasn't."

Indeed, the Tipplers can attest to the restorative magic of the seven-piece plate from the "Chef Paul's House of Wings" menu, served until last call, whenever that may be. But with every drink order named as a food on the receipt, it's not surprising that, under Louisiana law, Call is considered a restaurant rather than a bar. The benefit of this designation is that, despite the fact that the Last Call appears to be more of a bar and is only spitting distance from Bourbon Street, the establishment must be smoke free.

The Last Call is brighter than the average dive, a no-attitude sort of place with a simple wooden bar and tables, a mishmash of college pennants on the walls, and, most nights, football on four televisions—a relatively small number for the Quarter. The games don't overpower the jukebox, which is, frankly, more to the Tipplers' taste than most, and the music doesn't overpower conversation. Tonight there's a good mix of tourists and locals, including an infant.

As Elizabeth downs her beer, she keeps looking in the direction of the giant boxing-glove machine. It's pretty clear she isn't going to be able to resist "The Glove" for much longer. For a mere dollar, you can punch it and have your strength scaled.

"That's it," she says and slides off her stool. She puts in her dollar. The massive glove lowers. Taking aim, she fires. The screen flashes. Visibly disgruntled, she reads out the decision: *Anemic.*

As the Tipplers finish up their shots, a man wearing a chicken costume waddles in from Conti Street and walks to the end of the bar. He removes the oversized yellow and red head, puts down his Chef Paul's House of Wings poster, then bends down and slips off the bricklike red fleece slippers. The fake fur has left him in a visible sweat.

The bartender rushes over with a bottle of water. "You got to hydrate, Dave."

Sorry, but we can't resist this one: could it be Dave's last caw?

Name: Ninth Circle

Address: 700 North Rampart Street (at St. Peter Street)

Phone: 504-524-7654

Your tab: Who knows? Who cares? By the time you get here, you're not going to be able to keep track.

What you're swilling: Something in a glass, or a cup, or a can (see above). All we can say for sure is that it'll be wet, probably.

What you're wearing: A loincloth, maybe a tuxedo—in this dim lighting, we can't see too well.

What you're hearing: Great music on the speaker that you won't remember the next morning

Tattoo themes: Anything goes, and it'll all be on display.

Your drinking buddies: Men and women who've had a little too much of everything

Best feature: The fact that nobody's going to judge you or hold you accountable for anything done here

Decades ago, places like the Ninth Circle were called "dens of sin." Now, people just call them "seedy," which is shorter, filthier, and more apropos.

The Ninth Circle doesn't truly get hopping until late in the evening—or early in the morning, depending on your circadian rhythm. In fact, it's got such a late start time that the three of us have trouble coordinating our schedules to get here. We keep falling asleep, or passing out. When we finally get our acts together and show up en masse, we find that we're still too early. It's just past midnight, and there's not much of a crowd yet. The music is great, though, so we order a few beers at the bar and give the other patrons a once-over.

There are a couple of young men in the corner, macking on each other like it's their first date (ah, young love). Down the bar, there's a drag queen engaged in rapt conversation with a gentleman of a certain age. And two giddy women saunter off towards the bathroom, hand in hand. They don't return for a very long time.

Over the next 30 minutes, people come and go. It's like a very slow day at Grand Central Station: small groups of weary revelers wander in, grab a drink, hit the restroom, then bounce right out the door. Another group shows up to take their place, then another, and another. Apart from the couple still tongue wrestling in the corner, the crowd changes every 15 minutes. The Ninth Circle is a pit stop, a pick-me-up for partiers.

Weirdly, even though none of us has done anything illicit— not tonight, anyway—we feel perkier, too. It's energy by osmosis, and it's just the push we need to get back out the door and home again.

Name: The Three Legged Dog
Address: 400 Burgundy Street
Phone: 504-412-8335
Your tab: Five dollars for a draft beer, if it's working; generous well pours for six dollars
What you're swilling: Something from a plastic cup
What you're wearing: A hazmat suit and rubber gloves
What you're hearing: Mark Harmon
When you're there: When you feel the need to hit rock bottom and/or eat gravy fries. Pub grub is available.
Tattoo themes: Barbed wire
Your drinking buddies: The brave and the reckless
Best feature: To be decided

In the spirit of full disclosure, we should probably admit something right now. When we began this project, we felt inclined to add a rung beneath the low-rung category of "dive," like the gutter beneath the sidewalk. We labeled this level "dissolute." At the time it seemed like a good idea.

Of course, New Orleans has always made space for the lowest rung. It's one of the things we're known for. And perhaps the Tipplers' perverse interest in the dissolute stems from our city's fascination with decay, already duly noted by many writers. It may also come from the fact that we live in the subtropics or *the fungal zone.* So we're not afraid of a little dirt. We're old friends with germs, mold, vermin, and odors especially. Anyone who has walked through the French Quarter is well acquainted with the nuances of human markings that shift from step to step.

If you're thinking, *I bet this is foreshadowing,* you get a gold star.

Very few parts of the Quarter feel quiet, even fewer *desolate,* but at 8:00 P.M. on a Tuesday in early autumn, the 400-500 blocks of Burgundy feel exactly that. In all fairness, this is a mostly residential section, but the shuttered and lightless shotguns and Creole cottages along this stretch feel uncharacteristically abandoned tonight. Indeed we're not even convinced that our destination, the Three Legged Dog, is open. Unlike most of the bars on our list, this one is unfamiliar territory for us.

We step past a sofa, eviscerated and lying on its side, now reduced to a curbside corpse. It feels like the point in the movie where you shout at the hapless couple on the screen, "Turn around! Go back!" But of course, like the couple in the film, we keep going. The story depends on it. *It'll be okay*, we tell ourselves. *How bad can it be?*

We step through the Dutch door and see that it affords the Three Legged Dog's only view of the street. At first, it's difficult to differentiate the browns—ceiling, walls, floor. However, we immediately note a first for the Tipplers: not a single sports event is being shown on the televisions. "NCIS" plays on all four screens. What's more, we can actually hear the show, since there's no conversation or jukebox to compete with the sound. As a friend comments, sports cable costs more than regular channels. The draft beer is all down, and there's a distinct smell of bilging sewage—hard times indeed.

In the hour we are there, a total of three other patrons, all male and alone, come to drink. One of them turns out not to be a customer but an employee or owner. Another is dispatched by the barmaid to fetch menthols; as he rises from his stool, we realize he is carrying a sleeping roll. The third drinker exits with: "See ya. I got *shites* to deal with!" He hoists a hefty bag over his shoulder, a bag that may contain garbage (because, of course, that's what you bring to a bar), his belongings, or, say, body parts. The "NCIS" episode is not helping. As we watch Mark Harmon bend down to examine the latest victim, we thank New Orleans for go-cups.

Here are some final thoughts, made from a distance:

1. We applaud the honesty and limping implicit in the bar's name.

2. It is very unlikely that we will ever drink here with our mothers.

3. Contrary to popular belief, it is not *always* happy hour at the Three Legged Dog. Our plastic-cup whiskey and sodas were

ample but cost six bucks each. The draft beer was all down.

4. Sadly, there were no visible underpants stuck to the ceiling as promised by multiple reviewers, only dollar bills and what appeared to be a fairly recent coat of brown paint.

5. The number of visible, fully adult cockroaches present in the bar exceeded the number of humans.

6. At this time, concerns over safety prevent testing the supposed superior quality of the bathroom graffiti.

7. Our conclusion is that the Three Legged Dog belongs to the few, the brave—indeed, the *very* brave—and the dissolute.

CHAPTER 7

LGBT Bars

New Orleans is more tolerant than many places in America. Do you want to start drinking at 10:00 A.M.? We're not going to judge. Do you want to walk around dressed like a Viking one weekday afternoon? Knock yourself out. This acceptance has helped create a place where lesbians, gays, bisexuals, and transgendered individuals can build community. Long before gay bars were common in America, New Orleans had several. (In fact, prior to Storyville's experiment in legalized prostitution in the late 19th century, there were gay brothels in parts of the city.)

That's not to say that the LGBT community has always had it easy here. In 1973, an arsonist set fire to the UpStairs Lounge, a gay bar at the upper end of the Quarter. Thirty-two patrons were killed. Some families were so ashamed, they refused to collect the remains of their loved ones, and the first clergyman to host a prayer ceremony honoring the victims was barraged with hate mail.

But on the whole, the city has taken a live-and-let-live approach to LGBT matters. Maybe it's our laissez-faire European roots or the fact that we're a port city that's seen it all. Whatever the reason, New Orleans has an abundance of bars for the LGBT community. Like in many other cities, the bars are heavily geared towards gay men, but you'll find more than a few places for the transgendered, too. Lesbians are less obviously represented, but look closely at places such as the Bourbon Pub and Good Friends, and you'll find them as well.

Name: 700 Club
Address: 700 Burgundy Street (at St. Peter Street)
Phone: 504-561-1095
Web site: www.700ClubNewOrleans.com
Your tab: Very manageable, even for specialty drinks
What you're swilling: Whatever you like, but the martinis are awfully good.
What you're wearing: Jeans and a T-shirt, clubwear, formal attire—take your pick. No one's going to give you flack.
What you're hearing: It varies, but there's likely to be something with a good beat on the speaker. We give it a "10," because you can probably dance to it.
Tattoo themes: They vary, but since this is a pretty local joint, you should expect to see more than a few fleurs-de-lis. Tribal tats aren't uncommon, either.
Your drinking buddies: Mostly local gay men and lesbians. There's a slightly twinkish (i.e., "young and clubby") vibe, but it's not overwhelming.
Best feature: It's a great place for conversation, and the bar food is better than you'd expect.

New Orleans' gay nightlife is centered around the "Fruit Loop," which is not, in fact, a loop at all. It's an *L*-shaped series of bars that runs up Bourbon Street from Cafe Lafitte in Exile to the Bourbon Pub and Oz, then down St. Ann to Good Friends and Rawhide. As party promoters will tell you, prying gays out of the Fruit Loop for events elsewhere in the Quarter—much less the city—can be like pulling teeth.

That doesn't mean that people aren't looking for other places to hang out. Everyone needs a break now and then from the rowdy crowds on the strip, and for that, 700 Club is a great option.

Thankfully, 700 is a mere hop, skip, and a sashay from the Fruit Loop shenanigans. In fact, it's only two half-blocks (or one full block) from Rawhide, but it feels a world away. And that's why we've come here: to rest our feet and get a little sustenance.

Yes, 700 Club has food, and it's good—far better than at some French Quarter restaurants we could name. We ask for an order of fries, some onion rings, and two plates of chicken sliders. That ought to do the trick.

But before our food arrives, the youngish man next to us offers some advice. "Sugar, did you get the fried mac and cheese?"

No, we did not.

"Honey, you don't know what you're missing. Here," he says, shoving a plate in our direction. "I can't eat another bite if I'm going to stay in these jeans. Not that I'm trying to, but you know." He cocks his head and grins mischievously.

If we were younger, we'd probably tell the guy, "Thanks, but no thanks." After all, this seems awfully close to accepting candy from strangers. But we're older now, not to mention tipsier and hungrier. We also know the secret that our parents and teachers kept hidden all those years: a stranger's just a friend you haven't met.

We make the right choice by sampling his plate: the deep-fried mac and cheese is worth the price of admission (not that there's an admission charge, mind you). We ask for three more orders and thank our lucky stars that none of us is wearing jeans tonight.

Photograph by John d'Addario

Name: Bourbon Pub & Parade
Address: 801 Bourbon Street (at St. Ann Street)
Phone: 504-529-2107
Web site: www.BourbonPub.com
Your tab: Entirely manageable. Sunday is made for socializing on the cheap, with the time-honored tradition of Tea Dance, upstairs at the Parade.
What you're swilling: Everything's up for grabs—though generally speaking, you're going to be drinking out of plastic, so if you're picky about your martinis, opt for something else. Like at most other Bourbon Street boîtes, expect to see a lot of shots passed around.
What you're wearing: A mix of jeans, shorts, khakis, and clubwear. Unless you're still doing the Seattle-circa-1992 grunge thing, you ought to feel right at home.
What you're hearing: Lots of dance music on the speaker, and it tends to get loud. (But then, you're on Bourbon Street. What'd you expect?) Some nights are all about show tunes (Wednesday); others feature oldies (Sunday). And if you're feeling really brave, there's karaoke at the Parade on Thursday. We won't see you there.
Tattoo themes: All over the map, from tiny cartoon figures to Celtic armbands to classic Japanese sleeves. Since there are plenty of locals afoot, you'll glimpse lots of fleurs-de-lis, too.
Your drinking buddies: A swirl of New Orleanians, blended with an equal number of tourists. The crowd tends to be around 70 percent male—sometimes more—with an emphasis on preppy and twink types, but the demographic varies from night to night.
Best feature: The downstairs bar is great for an afternoon drink, but the balcony overlooking Bourbon wins first prize.

We're upstairs at the Bourbon Pub, which is technically called the Parade. And we've huddled at the corner of the balcony for one of the best free shows in town.

It's Saturday night, and Bourbon Street is in full-throated

roar 15 feet below. The dance tracks blaring onto the sidewalk beneath us mix with the jazz from Fritzel's a few doors down and a thousand other tunes, all doing their best to compete with hundreds of college kids screaming at one another in monosyllables:

"Dude!"

"I am so drunk!"

"Dude, I know!"

"Like, dude."

"Dude."

But as amusing and schadenfreudy as it is to look down upon younguns enjoying their fleeting moments on the world's most debauched boulevard, we're watching something entirely different. Because here, at the intersection of Bourbon and St. Ann, is an invisible wall. It discreetly divides "straight" Bourbon Street from a handful of bars that cater to LGBT clientele. Bourbon doesn't look much different on the gay side—the bars are just as brightly lit and boisterous as they are a few yards upstream, and the crowds are equally giddy and tipsy. So what's the tipoff?

Maybe it's the rainbow flags fluttering from the balconies. Maybe it's the music, which is decidedly more thumpa-thumpa-wailing-disco-diva than the pop-radio craptracks heard at joints farther up Bourbon. It might even be the drag queens congregating on the corner, cutting up over cocktails.

But really, we don't question the "why" of the invisible wall. We just know that it's there, and people bump into it as if it's a force field in a bad sci-fi movie. *Zap!*

"Dude, come back!"

Zap!

The Bourbon Pub & Parade are an unusual mix of Bourbon Street nightclub and local hangout. Step through the inviting French doors, and you're just as likely to meet someone from Nigeria or Nicaragua as next door.

Downstairs at the Pub, most of the floorspace is taken up

by a gigantic square bar set into the middle of the room, with service on all four sides. On weekends, the atmosphere is jovial and festive, but the best time to enjoy the Pub might be in the afternoon. Before the nighttime crowds arrive, it's a great place to nurse a spicy bloody mary after a long day of conventioneering or before a pre-dinner nap.

But tonight, we're here to shake a few tail feathers, and for that, we've come up to the Parade. It features a good-size dance floor, which gets pleasantly packed during the wee hours. Sometimes, it hosts drag shows and less family-friendly fare, especially during Mardi Gras and the Southern Decadence Festival.

After a few songs and a lot of sweat, we grab a third (or maybe fourth) round of cocktails and head back to the balcony to cool off. A group of tourists have taken our spot at the corner, leaning against the iron railing and watching the invisible wall in action below. They laugh, and we laugh at their delight. We're getting two great shows, and they're both free.

Name: Cafe Lafitte in Exile
Address: 901 Bourbon Street (at Dumaine Street)
Phone: 504-522-8397
Web site: www.Lafittes.com
Your tab: Very bearable—until you start throwing back the shots, that is. But by that time, do you really give a damn?
What you're swilling: Entirely your call, though the bartenders can make you something special, if you're feeling indecisive.
What you're wearing: Lafitte's (or "Fifi's," as it's occasionally known) has a reputation as being a bar for the scruffy, Levi's-wearing set—and it is, to a degree, but not nearly as much as its leathery sibling, Rawhide. Jeans, shorts, T-shirts: these are the best costumes for the day.
What you're hearing: Pop, dance, and other peppy tunes on the speaker
Tattoo themes: Lafitte's attracts a multigenerational crowd, and the ink on view proves it. Rainbow triangles, Celtic armbands, icons made popular by Pink Floyd and Led Zeppelin: they're all on display here.
Your drinking buddies: Bourbon Street bars are typically the province of under-30 revelers. But because Cafe Lafitte sits at the tail end of the touristy part of the street—and because it's a decades-old institution—men of all ages feel comfortable hanging out there. Look closely, and you might even spot a drag queen and a RG (i.e., "real girl") or two.
Best feature: Like Oz, the Bourbon Pub, and many other French Quarter bars, Cafe Lafitte sits on a corner, and it has a wraparound balcony, which is great. But the best feature of Lafitte's is just inside the front door: the gaslight known as the eternal flame. Please don't use it as a cigarette lighter.

Cafe Lafitte in Exile is a great place to chat, though given the heavy dance beats pumping through the sound system, that's easier to do outside than at the bar. Oftentimes, we grab our drinks and slip out to the sidewalk, where the crowd bubbles into the street.

But tonight, we're heading upstairs to catch a benefit for a local nonprofit.

In previous years, the fundraiser's main event was "red bean wrestling," which was exactly what you'd think: a bunch of tipsy guys getting grungy in an inflatable swimming pool full of canned legumes.

Then one year, just for kicks, the organizers decided to fill the pool with ravioli instead, which was a disappointment. For starters, ravioli doesn't have the same New Orleans cachet that red beans do. But more importantly, canned ravioli reeks like hell. You know that tangy, metallic-meets-metal scent you get when you crack open a can of Chef Boyardee? Imagine it on an industrial scale. The wrestling was as hilarious as always, but no one could really enjoy it because we were all trying hard not to vomit.

Thankfully, the folks in charge recently changed the wrestling substance again, this time to "personal lubricant." It's just as slimy as ravioli but without the God-awful stench. We consider it a sexy win-win.

Unfortunately, by the time the three of us arrive upstairs, the place is packed. We can't even get close to the kiddie pool where the wrestlers are duking it out, so we head out to the balcony for a little fresh air, hoping that a spot near the action will open up later. Across Bourbon Street, Lafitte's is projecting a music video onto the wall of Clover Grill. None of us recognizes the artist—or rather, "artist."

About that time, a car drives by with its windows down, blaring an old Kylie Minogue track with a catchy refrain: "I just can't get you out of my head, boy. Your lovin' is all I think about." Even people who don't know the song very well are familiar with the chorus, which is an endless series of "la la las." Conversations halt midsentence as everyone pauses to sing along: "So there I was, with a martini in one hand and a cigarette in the other—la, la, la, la, la, la, la, la, la, la, la, la, la, la, la, la—when guess who walked in!"

Half an hour down the road, the bar is twice as crowded. We push towards the stairs in hopes of glimpsing at least one lubed-up wrestler from a distance, but alas, it's not to be. We head back out into the night, thankful that the nonprofit has made some cash and that our clothes don't stink of canned tomato sauce. All in all, it's an auspicious start to the night.

Name: The Corner Pocket
Address: 940 St. Louis Street (at Burgundy Street)
Phone: 504-568-9829
Web site: www.CornerPocket.net
Your tab: Cheap; cash only. (Also, bring singles. You'll understand why pretty quickly.)
What you're swilling: The simpler things in life: beer and cocktails with no more than three components (gin and tonic, Jack and Coke). Don't expect fruit (in your drink).
What you're wearing: Anything you like, though dressing down isn't a bad idea. Whatever you're sporting, you'll be overdressed compared to the dancers on the bar, unless you're the sort of person who hits the town in a thong.
What you're hearing: Bass-heavy dance music on the speaker, with a tendency towards techno
Tattoo themes: On the patrons: fleur-de-lis. (Yes, it's mostly locals in the crowd.) On the dancers: crosses, skulls, and the names of girlfriends who may or may not know about their man's sideline. Some of the dancers' ink looks, shall we say, homemade.
Your drinking buddies: Mostly gay men of a certain age, but also younger ones, and a reasonable crowd of straight folks. Everyone's here to be entertained, but everyone also has different ideas about what constitutes entertainment.
Best feature: The scene around the pool table at the rear of the place. It's like a life-size diorama you'd find in a natural history museum, except these cavemen are still breathing—mostly.

When you cross Bourbon Street, moving away from the river, everything changes a little. There are fewer people and fewer lights. Well, okay, technically there are plenty of people, but they don't look like tourists. They seem more like . . . fixtures. You keep walking down the block; they stay put. They've already been around a few times.

Long before we reach the Corner Pocket, we hear the music

Photograph by John d'Addario

thumping. (Note to self: do *not* rent that charming shotgun apartment next door.) Listening closely, we can almost make out the voice of a drag queen on the bar's ratty P.A. system, hoarsely shouting over the *disco tragique*. Here at the corner of St. Louis and Burgundy streets, even with the relentless bass line hammering through the shuttered windows, the sidewalk is relatively quiet—just a couple of younger guys hang out in front of the bar, talking. But open the door, and it's a different world.

The lighting inside is pleasant-ish, indirect and neon. The crowd is sizable. It's 11:00 P.M. now, and humanity (heavy on the "man") has packed itself around the rectangular bar that takes up the middle of the room. Not to wax poetic, but it's kind of an oasis of flesh—like Bourbon Street just 100 yards ago but somehow more palatable. It's debauched in a civil sort of way.

It's Friday, which means it's New Meat Night, featuring a dance contest open to interested patrons. We hand our five-dollar cover charges to the nice guy at the door and belly up to the bar for a drink. There are no frills on display. This is not the kind of place for froufrou and paper umbrellas. Some of the silver-haired gentlemen perched elegantly on stools may look as if they'd order a grasshopper or a pink squirrel (old schoolers still exist), but no, most are content with a beer, or a gin and tonic, or a bourbon and soda. That simplicity is reflected in the rock-bottom prices, which in turn mean more drinks for you and more dollar bills for the people on top of the bar.

Yes, there are people on top of the bar, specifically, young people, and more specifically, thin-to-athletic young men in underwear, athletic socks, and sneakers, many of whom possess a special talent for gyrating. Every so often, the tranny emcee in the corner shouts into her microphone, announcing a new dancer in the contest: Ramon, or Charlie, or Sven, from Lafayette, or Latvia, or Terre Haute. They mount the bar—some aggressively, some just barely—and over the course of one blaring techno ditty that sounds remarkably like the one that played before it, the young men slink their way around the rectangle, stopping every few feet to encourage patronage in their own special way. Tips are appreciated, visibly.

(Legend has it that this is where filmmaker John Waters first saw the stripper move known as "teabagging," wherein a male dancer drags his dangly parts—modestly contained by tighty-whiteys, of course—across the heads of favored patrons. If you need a visual, rent *Pecker*.)

We grab our drinks and mosey to the back of the room, where a group of young men clad only in skivvies and shoes wait for their bar-top turn, playing pool and smoking. A few gentlemen cast lascivious glances at the dancers, but it's mostly lighthearted. There's something about the Corner Pocket that's so over the top and self-aware that the place (generally) avoids being sleazy. Sure, there are some who've come for the sexual thrills, but far more patrons have popped in for the campy spectacle of it all. A handful of others just enjoy cheap drinks, loud music, and the company of friends.

Despite the fact that the crowd is primarily gay, the vibe is straight-friendly. In fact, you can see more than a few straight couples sprinkled around the room. That's pretty standard: for many locals, taking out-of-towners to the Corner Pocket is a raucous, hilarious way to introduce visitors to the city we call home. Then again, they could just be looking for that special third wheel.

Back on the bar, the contest drags on, and on, and on. We are barraged by an endless wave of Pretty Young Things, all waiting for a chance to bump, grind, and teabag themselves a little closer towards rent, the electric bill, and a Clover Grill hamburger with chili cheese fries. (Yes, they'll regret that in the morning, too.) At one point, it appears that things are winding down, but no one seems to know how to put an end to it. As the drag queen rambles into her cheap microphone, we make our way towards the exit. Many other patrons linger, hoping to get lucky, but we've seen plenty already. We don't want to push our luck.

Name: The Double Play
Address: 439 Dauphine Street (at St. Louis Street)
Phone: 504-523-4517
Your tab: Cheap
What you're swilling: Low-key fare such as beer and two-ingredient cocktails. This ain't no party; this ain't no disco.
What you're wearing: Whatever you like, but most everyone else will be dressed down.
What you're hearing: A mix of jukebox fare, with a tendency towards festive tunes
Tattoo themes: All over the map, but given the bar's unpretentious tone, customers aren't often showing it off.
Your drinking buddies: The Double Play is about as working-class as LGBT bars get, so the crowd is usually low-key.
Best feature: If you want a behind-the-scenes look at the Quarter's daily gay life—warts and all—this is the place to get it.

If we had wanted to, we could have classified the Double Play as a neighborhood bar. Aside from the fact that most of the folks who drink here are gay men, the place feels like countless other corner pubs: casual, friendly, and decidedly no-nonsense. But the sexual orientation of the Double Play's clientele is important, as is the average age of those at the bar. It's not the kind of joint that twinks and other Bright Young Things visit on a regular basis. It's not the kind of place with music cranked so high you can't hear yourself think. It is, however, the perfect spot to sit and talk when the other bars become a little overwhelming.

And that's what has led us here. After an hour on Bourbon Street, we're dizzy from an assortment of well-brand shots, which were served with a raucous mix of rock, jazz, disco, and karaoke. As Streisand once said, enough is freakin' enough.

The Double Play is quiet, but like a safe room, not a wake. As the door shuts behind us, the roar of the crowd one block away goes silent. It's paradise.

The bartender rustles up a quick round of drinks: two vodka

tonics and one bourbon, neat (to fight off the unseasonably chilly March night). We start to chat quietly, but our ears are ringing, and for all we know, we might be shouting.

Before long, the guy sitting next to Richard swivels to face us. He cocks his head to one side and says, "Honey, you think it's cold tonight? You should've been out at My-O-My on the lakefront. Even in May, that'd freeze your tits off."

We can't tell if the man was one of the legendary female impersonators at the Club My-O-My—which entertained straights and gays alike for decades, until it burned in 1972—or if he was just an occasional patron. But he's a good storyteller, and really, that's all that matters.

Thirty minutes later, during a lull in the conversation, we thank him for sharing his tales about gay life in New Orleans before and after the 1969 Stonewall Inn raid in New York. Warm and revived, we bundle up and brace ourselves for louder bars to come.

Name: Golden Lantern

Address: 1239 Royal Street

Phone: 504-529-2860

Your tab: Cheaper than Bourbon Street but with the same assortment of booze

What you're swilling: Beer and basics such as rum and Coke or gin and tonic are common, but no one's going to blink if you order a sidecar.

What you're wearing: Anything is A-Okay, though it bears mentioning that this is largely a neighborhood bar. Arrive in a shirt and tie, and people might think you're uppity.

What you're hearing: Depending on the crowd, the very well stocked jukebox can bounce from rock to oldies to New Wave in the course of an hour. Don't get too attached.

Tattoo themes: Given the Golden Lantern's slightly older clientele, you're likely to glimpse some ink that predates the tribal designs that dominated the '90s and '00s. (Think Ziggy and Led Zeppelin.) There may even be a couple of military tats in the bunch.

Your drinking buddies: Mostly locals, mostly gay, mostly from the Quarter and the adjacent Faubourg Marigny. Tourists are more than welcome, but the vibe here is neighborhoody. If you're looking for a full-on party, this may not be the place for you.

Best feature: The occasional drag shows are hilarious, though often unintentionally so. These are not the great female impersonators found in Las Vegas floor shows; these are mom-and-pop (mostly pop) drag queens, attempting to lip-synch for a few extra bucks. The Christmas Eve extravaganza is as close as you'll ever get to a bacchanal like the one depicted in John Waters' *Pink Flamingos*.

Elizabeth likes to tell the story of how years ago, when she first moved downtown, she and her roommate, Brian, called the Golden Lantern and tried to order takeout. "We thought it was a Chinese restaurant," she explains with a shrug and a giggle.

If only they had stepped inside. Despite the name, there's no chinoiserie in the Golden Lantern. In fact, it's a pitch-perfect French Quarter bar: exposed brick, dim lighting, and a worn wooden bar top, typically ringed by a bevy of folks from the surrounding gay-borhood, dishing about the latest local news.

We enter on a warm, muggy summer night, instantly soothed by a blast from the Lantern's high-octane air-conditioning. The front room is about half-full—which isn't saying too much, since it's on the small side. A dozen patrons are perched on stools, tossing 'em back. Another pair plays video poker.

The Lantern draws a fairly "mature" crowd, but for some reason, the music pumping through the speakers tonight is pure contemporary pop—a series of regrettable one-hit wonders performed by groups lost in the mists of the early 2000s. After a few minutes, we spot the culprit across the bar: a local guy with a reputation for dominating the jukebox for hours on end. He's nodding in time to Ace of Base and lip-synching to no one in particular. As Heidi Klum would say, we question his taste level. We sigh in unison.

We grab an assortment of drinks—one Abita, one margarita, one martini (extra dirty)—and slip to the back room, which isn't so much towards the back as to the side. It was recently renovated, and it looks brand-spankin' new compared to the well-worn front. But despite not being broken in, it's comfy, which is really all we're looking for: a place to cool down and catch our breath before soldiering on, leaving the Spice Girls and their ill-begotten ilk behind.

A drink and a half later, the crowd begins encroaching on our turf. There's a drag show a-comin'. This ought to be good: the Golden Lantern attracts some of the oldest queens in captivity, few of whom ever bother to memorize the words to the songs they're lip-synching.

But there's a difference between bad-good and just plain bad. One of tonight's performers is so sloppy, she can't even remember the words to Patsy Cline's "Crazy," which everyone else in the bar can sing in their sleep. Richard grabs a stack of napkins and starts scribbling cue cards, but before he can put them to use, Allison and Elizabeth gently guide him towards the exit. Better to walk out than be thrown out, we suppose.

Photograph by John d'Addario

Name: Good Friends Bar

Address: 740 Dauphine Street (at St. Ann Street)

Phone: 504-566-7191

Web site: www.GoodFriendsBar.com

Your tab: Manageable but not inexpensive. (Though remember: "manageable" in New Orleans = *"OMG, it costs nothing to get hammered here!"* to people from other cities. We're a cheap date.)

What you're swilling: As long as you don't get too high and mighty, the cuties on duty should have what you want. Beer abounds, but if you're going to order a pink squirrel or a grasshopper anywhere in town, you might as well do it at Good Friends: no one will look at you funny. If it's hot outside—and it probably is—ask for a frozen separator, which is, as you might imagine, like a separator, but frozen. (NB: A separator is basically a White Russian with brandy instead of vodka. And it's brilliant.)

What you're wearing: Good Friends' tagline is: "Always snappy casual." Of course, "snappy casual" means one thing at 3:00 P.M. on a Sunday and quite another at 5:00 A.M. on a Monday. No one's going to throw you out if you schlep in with cutoffs and flip-flops, but standing beneath the bar's neon ferns, you might feel more comfy in chinos and a polo.

What you're hearing: Happy-shiny-people dance music on the speaker, though the volume's usually low enough to hold a conversation with your friends (if you don't mind shouting a little)

Tattoo themes: The crowd here is a tad too old for tats—or at least, too old to bear fully inked sleeves. You're more likely to see the occasional tribal/barbed-wire armband or a fleur-de-lis on the back of someone's calf. Facial tattoos may generate stares and winces of pain.

Your drinking buddies: Gay men of a certain age, twinks who've come to hang with their friends behind the bar, and a reasonable assortment of straight women partying with same. Most are on good behavior.

Best feature: Upstairs, hands down. Go in the afternoon so you can grab a seat under one of the umbrellas on the balcony. Do some people-watching, but for goodness sakes, please don't try to offer any beads to the passersby unless you're visiting for Carnival.

It's Sunday, and the weather is beautiful, with just the tiniest of chills in the air. We're not stupid: we know that chill will hang around for five more minutes before Mother Nature plunges us headlong into summer. Spring in New Orleans is like the antechamber you pass through on the way to the can in fancy hotels: brief and perfunctory. Blink and you'll miss it. But while it's here, we head over to Good Friends to live it up.

Since it's not quite hot enough for frozen separators—Good Friends' signature drink—Allison and Elizabeth order whiskey (neat, please). Richard, for some reason, is on a bitters-and-soda binge. It must be something he ate. At least they have Angostura on hand, which is richer and fuller than the locally made Peychaud's.

We try to pay the bartender, but he ignores us. Well, he's not ignoring us per se; he's just not in a hurry to see us leave. We're nicely dressed and, more importantly, we look like good tippers. He wagers (correctly) that we're not the type to drink and dash.

We talk, which is something we can do in Good Friends, unlike the bars a block away on Bourbon Street. There, it's as if the management tries to vibrate customers out the door with loud bass beats to make room for the next wave of boozers.

Good Friends isn't so far off the tourist route as to be obscure—in fact, it's on the Fruit Loop. But despite its location, Good Friends feels like a neighborhood bar. And that's because it is. Sure, there are tourists in the corners, looking confused—"Is that a staircase? Can we go up there? Do they make hurricanes?"—but the crowd is mostly local. It's divvied up into small groups of friends just like us, clumped together and toasting the end of another well-deserved weekend.

We exchange pleasantries with the couple to our left—two guys Richard knew a lifetime ago who now live out in the 'burbs. We watch the music videos, which typically feature taut pop tartlets we've never heard of, though occasionally the VJ throws in a classic ditty to vary things up. Someone in the corner is playing a trivia game on one of the big screens; he's clearly stumped by a question about '60s movie stars. "Steve McQueen!" a helpful patron shouts across the bar. Bingo. A shot is sent over in thanks.

As the sun sets, we debate where to go next. We They could go upscale and visit the Carousel Bar at the Monteleone, but it's a hike and it's crowded on Sunday afternoons (even with the bar's recent expansion). Or we could go downmarket and hit Decatur Street.

But Good Friends is one of those places you want to end up, the bar you want to visit last. It's like that final, perfect bite of bread pudding or sip of a snowball (blackberry with condensed milk, please!), the taste you want to linger in your mouth before you push back from the table and say, "I'm done." It's a boozy Venn diagram where comfort and companions and cost overlap, and there's nowhere to go after that.

Name: Le Roundup
Address: 819 St. Louis Street
Phone: 504-561-8430
Your tab: Cheap. This is a drinker's bar, and the prices prove it.
What you're swilling: Whatever you want, so long as it's simple. Get frou-frou, and you might get the stinkeye.
What you're wearing: Anything more demure than a G-string is fine. But then, who wants to be demure?
What you're hearing: There's a jukebox that pumps out a wide range of tunes, but dance ditties are the most popular. If you like Britney, Celine, and/or Cher, you're in the right place.
Tattoo themes: There are plenty of tats on display, but they're too diverse to classify by theme. Some patrons show off professional ink, while others might've done the work themselves.
Your drinking buddies: Le Roundup is a home base for hardworking French Quarter types looking to play a game of pool after the dinner shift. The clientele falls pretty squarely into the LGBT camp, with more than a few drag queens, transsexuals, and transvestites afoot. (If you don't know the difference, please school yourself before arrival.)
Best feature: The bar itself is pretty featureless, but the clientele aren't going to bother you if you don't want to be bothered. That's gotta count for something.

Entering through Le Roundup's swinging door, we feel as if we've stepped into a bad Western (appropriate, given the bar's name). The music on the jukebox suddenly stops, and everyone turns to give us the once-over.

Thankfully, that's as Western as it gets. As the next song revs up, the bartender waves us to a group of stools at the far end of the bar: "C'mon in, shug. What can I get ya?" Sixty seconds later, it's as though we're part of the family.

Le Roundup is like the Platonic ideal of drinking in the Quarter (though not so high-minded as Plato). There's no live music, no karaoke machine, and no chalkboard full of cocktails du jour. Without all that frippery, patrons can get right down to business: drinking, talking, playing pool, and eavesdropping on other conversations, like the one taking place across the bar between a tall woman and a much younger guy in a sleeveless undershirt.

"I'm just sayin', honey," she purrs, taking a sip of something pink. "Use it while you're young." She strokes his bicep with a long fingertip.

"Uh huh."

"I promise, it's not hard." She giggles and looks playfully at his lap. "Or is it?"

"Huh."

Then something loud and disco-y comes on the jukebox. "Girl, this is my jam!" the woman shouts to no one in particular, leaning back on her stool, palms planted firmly on the bar. She proceeds to lip-synch the entire song, getting most of the words right—no small feat given the fast pace. Whoever is singing sounds like Gloria Estefan in a helium factory, hopped up on 12 double espressos.

Finally, mercifully, the tune winds down, and the woman drags her young friend outside. We finish our drinks halfway through the next tune and decide to mosey on, secretly hoping to catch more of the couple's conversation. But by the time we walk into the crisp night air, all we can hear is the echo of the woman's laughter, bouncing off the stucco walls of St. Louis Street.

Name: Michael's on the Park
Address: 834 North Rampart Street
Phone: 504-267-3615
Web site: www.MichaelsOnThePark.com
Your tab: Not terrifically expensive. This is a place frequented mostly by locals, just a half-step up from what we'd consider a neighborhood bar. As a result, the drinks tend to be very fairly priced.
What you're swilling: Whatever you like, but since the vibe here is "neighborhoody," stick with something simple. If the bartenders have to look it up, it's not simple.
What you're wearing: Anything relaxed and casual. Like most bars in New Orleans (Napoleon's Itch being a notable exception), Michael's allows smoking, and when the place is packed, it can be a little overwhelming—especially for your clothes. Don't wear anything you can't wash the next day.
What you're hearing: A mix of pop and rock tunes from the jukebox—unless there's a drag show, in which case it's all up for grabs.
Tattoo themes: No particular theme, but you may notice a number of names (perhaps former boyfriends and girlfriends), cartoon characters, and other randomness lingering on forearms and around ankles.
Your drinking buddies: Men and women, mostly from the Quarter. The bulk are men, and many are—how should we say this?—mature. Depending on the night, there may be drag queens in abundance, but most are of the "weekend" variety, meaning that they probably wouldn't make the cut for a female impersonation revue.
Best feature: The back patio

Michael's sits at the edge of the French Quarter, on Rampart Street, which has seen some welcome changes in recent years. Not so long ago Rampart was what most people would call "sketchy," but since the '90s, residents of the Quarter and the neighboring Tremé have worked hard to reinvigorate this once-bustling street. And despite an abundance of lazy landlords and the occasional hurricane, their progress has been remarkable.

That said, Michael's is still homey. It's a far cry from the handful of gentrified joints found elsewhere on Rampart, boasting a decidedly low-key decor and an equally humble clientele. It's not unheard of for tourists to wander in, but it is rare.

We're fortunate enough to arrive in the middle of one of the bar's infamous drag shows. Most of the queens on display aren't in danger of "passing" (for women) anytime soon. In fact, some look manlier than the male patrons, even though they're dripping with bugle beads and rhinestones. But the crowd doesn't seem to mind: they're just happy to see their friends rouged up and having a good time.

We grab a few quick drinks—a couple of beers and a gin and tonic—then slide past the bar and pool table to the deck out back. Its only decor is a smattering of potted plants and some white Christmas lights. But the breeze is nice, and although we can still hear the music and hubbub from inside, it's quiet enough for conversation.

And that is what makes Michael's one of the most civilized bars in the Quarter. The bartenders may not make the best Pimm's cup in town. (Then again, maybe they do: we haven't tried ordering one.) And it may not have the most comfortable barstools. But for those who appreciate the difference between "drinking" and "partying," who need conversation to go along with their cocktails, there are few better places to hunker down.

Name: Napoleon's Itch
Address: 734 Bourbon Street (at St. Ann Street)
Phone: 504-237-4144
Web site: www.napoleonsitch.com
Your tab: The Itch offers a number of drink specials, including $3 well drinks ($2 on Tuesday "Ladys" nights) and $12 all you can drink from 8:00 to 10:00 P.M. In other words, it's cheap for Bourbon Street.
What you're swilling: Aside from cheap well drinks, consider a martini from their menu
What you're wearing: Tight jeans
What you're hearing: '70s and '80s pop by day, Shakira and Katy Perry by night on the speaker
When you're there: En route to somewhere else; however, the Itch is worth sticking around for a spell.
Tattoo themes: Tough to say with so few forearms in the place
Your drinking buddies: Sparse
Best feature: The Plexiglas with the changing mood colors behind the bar

Sometimes it may be best not to scratch beneath the surface. But if you must know about the name of the bar and Napoleon's reputation as a "passionate" lover, see the Web site. It won't help a bit, but you can try. The bathroom is spic and span, however, and given the name of the bar, that comes as a relief.

In terms of design, the Itch has a little dose of *je ne sais quoi*. As of the Tipplers' last venture in, we can count exactly two pieces of Napoleonic decor here—a framed print and a plastic bust on an appropriately petite piano. However, it is quite possible that the low ceilings (the bar is housed in the basement of the Bourbon Orleans Hotel) would have made the little emperor feel welcome.

If there's a phrase that best sums up the look here, it's not Napoleonic. Instead we settle on "Iron Curtain, circa glasnost"—

when a small trickle of Western items managed to find their way into Eastern Europe. Unlike most places in the Quarter, the Itch doesn't offer a cohesive look. To their credit, however, the staff recently shifted the furniture arrangement, and now patrons have several areas for conversation. The bar's best feature, a color play panel, finally gets the attention it deserves, and the young men who tend the bar look exceptionally pretty standing in its glow.

The Itch is less a destination bar than an easy refueling station or a spot for a quick round before dinner with a friend. By day, the Itch can verge on comatose. During the afternoon, you could easily pass an hour chatting with the friendly bartender and sipping a reasonably priced drink in a smoke-free spot while your partner fetches something from the hardware store. By night, the place becomes decidedly more clubby. And while the lack of a dance floor means that Napoleon's Itch is never packed like other locales on Bourbon, its poppy mixes, overhead videos, and light-up color panel offer a boost of energy for Tipplers in need of a comfy chair, a clean bathroom, and a timeout in order to chart their next move.

Name: Oz
Address: 800 Bourbon Street (at St. Ann Street)
Phone: 504-593-9491
Web site: www.OzNewOrleans.com
Your tab: Average, unless you go crazy with lemon drops, sex-on-the-beach shots, and other Bourbon Street fare, which would not be unheard of but might call for a trip to the ATM
What you're swilling: Anything you like, but remember: it's going to come in a plastic cup or a tin can, so don't get all fancypants.
What you're wearing: Sexy clubwear is a good place to start, though some people just show up in cargo shorts and T-shirts. (New Orleans' sultry climate results in a forgiving dress code.)
What you're hearing: A nonstop barrage of thumpa-thumpa dance beats. Seriously, this is ground zero for the style of music generally known as High NRG. The DJs get a little more adventurous and progressive as the evening wears on—and that goes double during High Gay Holy Days such as Halloween and Southern Decadence.
Tattoo themes: All over the map, but this is gay territory, so you'll see more than a handful of tribal armbands and other decorative ink. Confederate flags? Not so much.
Your drinking buddies: Mostly guys and their gal-pals. Oz caters to a slightly younger clientele than some other gay bars in New Orleans, so the crowd skews towards twinks and their admirers. Drag queens can often be found stomping to the beats, as well as a limited number of LGBT-friendly straight folk who've wandered in from the street. All in all, it's a convivial bunch.
Best feature: Like the Bourbon Pub across the street, Oz has a great wraparound balcony. But the large, ground-floor dance area is an oasis for those jonesing to shake their groove things.

As we walk up Bourbon Street from the Clover Grill (nothing like a quick meal of chili cheese fries to prep the stomach for a

Photograph by John d'Addario

night of cocktailing), we can't help noticing that the music blasting from Oz and the Bourbon Pub is almost indistinguishable. And in fact, since Oz opened in the early 1990s, revelers have been known to wander indiscriminately between the two. But Oz has its own character, thanks in part to its unique architecture. Long ago—long before it was Oz—someone put a roof over the building's courtyard. Today, that courtyard has become the dance floor, and the main building opens onto it, housing bars upstairs and down. That kind of grand flow is rare for a French Quarter bar, where buildings are usually constrained by 18th- and 19th-century architecture. As a result, Oz feels more like a booming, bigger-city nightclub than many others on the strip.

That said, drinking at Oz isn't all that different from drinking at other Bourbon Street bars. Beer and shots rule the day—or more commonly, the night. But a quick walk out to the balcony can put some distance between you and the hordes of tippling twinks and Spring Breakers.

This is exactly what we do. The night is clear, and even though it's the middle of summer, a pleasant breeze wafts up St. Ann from the river, carrying with it the scent of night-blooming jasmine. We park ourselves on the bench and gossip about our fellow drinkers—none of whom we know—critiquing the occasional costumed club kid who wanders by. (Who knew there were still club kids?)

Since it's Wednesday, there's a drag show at 10:30 P.M., so we dutifully step inside and peer down on the proceedings from what was once a balcony overlooking the courtyard/dance floor. The queens are in rare form tonight, shaking some perky numbers and putting the industrial-strength A/C system to very good use. When a friend of a friend gets pulled onstage and asked to show off his underwear, decorum forces us back to the balcony.

But as we step outside, we find a young woman, maybe college age, occupying our former seats. Given the way that she's lying half on, half off the bench, we guess she's had one too many. Richard taps her on the shoulder: "Ma'am, you ought to sit up. You're going to ruin that blouse."

To which she groggily responds, "It's a top, not a blouse."

Not one to be caught off guard, Richard fires back, "Believe me, sugar, I know a top when I see one. I hope you're not allergic to Woolite."

We leave the unappreciative tippler on the balcony and step back inside for another round—and maybe a dance or two.

Name: Rawhide

Address: 740 Burgundy Street (at St. Ann Street)

Phone: 504-525-8106

Web site: www.Rawhide2010.com

Your tab: Probably on the cheap side, since, like everyone else, you're likely to stick with beer

What you're swilling: Mostly stuff that comes from a keg or tin can—but hey, it's a free country.

What you're wearing: Prep-school fans may feel a little out of place here. To truly appreciate the vibe, you should at least show up in jeans, and leather is acceptable in cooler months. Accessorize with handkerchiefs.

What you're hearing: Seriously great music from the DJ, typically with a strong dance beat. It's on the loud side, but not so loud that you can't carry on a conversation—if you're here for conversation, that is.

Tattoo themes: Varied and abundant. Some people have obviously spent serious bucks on professionally inked sleeved. Others . . . well, others have gone the discount route. At least it's dark in here.

Your drinking buddies: Mostly guys, specifically: bears, leather daddies, and their many admirers. You'll see a few women here, too, but they're gravely outnumbered.

Best feature: Some folks enjoy the intimate back area of Rawhide, which is great for hanging out and making new friends. But the long bench in the front bar—called the "meat rack" in other places—is a perfect perch for people-watching.

I've left Allison and Elizabeth down the street. They haven't seen one another in a few weeks and need to catch up.

I need to catch up, too. I haven't been to Rawhide in a couple of months, and I want to see if anything's changed (highly unlikely, but just to be sure).

I could have brought the girls—heck, they've gamely tagged along to countless other gay bars. If they can handle Le Roundup, they can handle anything, right?

Maybe, maybe not. As you might guess from the name, Rawhide is a hangout favored by the bear/leather/Levi's set. It's not where you take your best girl friends for dancing. It's where you go when you're in the mood for a drink with the guys, or a date—sometimes, a very quick date.

It can get a little raunchy is what I'm saying.

And that's A-Okay by me. That's part of its allure. Not every bar is made for every kind of patron. So for Rawhide, I'm flying solo.

After the doorman checks my ID and I walk into the dim but artfully lit front room, I realize I needn't have been so overprotective. There are several women here, drinking and cutting up with their male companions. One plays pool; another stands by the bar, swaying to the music and chatting with friends.

It's about 10:00 P.M., so the place isn't too crowded yet. The long, low bench running the length of the front room is populated by a mix of local faces I recognize and a few guys in Bourbon Street T-shirts who might as well be wearing "I'm not from around these parts" neon medallions. The bulk of patrons are beary, or at least scruffy—though few have bothered to break out the leather, since it's the middle of July. Oh, the chafing.

Like at all bars in the Wood Enterprise family (including Good Friends and Cafe Lafitte in Exile), service at Rawhide is fast, friendly, and super-efficient. I opt for a beer, like most people in the place, but a quick glance at the liquor rack tells me they could accommodate an Alabama slammer or a Singapore sling if I had the nerve to order one. I don't.

I turn and survey the crowd once more. Everyone seems to be having a good time, enjoying the great music from the DJ. (Rawhide offers some of the best dance and techno music in the Quarter.) The videos aren't so bad either—if you like clips of hot, half-naked men, as I do.

Rawhide once had the reputation of being kind of a sex club, and to be sure, there's a good bit of groping and making out going on in the corners. But it's no racier than what you'd see at the Cat's Meow or Krazy Korner any day of the week. Things can get a little more titillating during festivals such as Southern Decadence and Mardi Gras—though again, that kind of thing isn't limited to gay bars.

The back of the club is dark and empty as I head to the can. I've seen couples getting hot and heavy in Rawhide's sleek, black-tiled bathroom, but tonight, it's just me, which is fine, since I'm a little shy.

I finish and head back up front. As I'm pouring the beer from its bottle into a go-cup, I run into a couple of friends I haven't seen in 10 years, maybe more. We chat for a few minutes, then drift away.

Yup, same old Rawhide, comfortable as a well-worn catcher's mitt, or a good pair of chaps.

CHAPTER 8

Hipster Bars

"Hipster" can be such an ugly word. What used to translate simply as "cool and edgy" has come to mean "trucker hats and scruffy beards," "style over substance," and, worst of all, "trendy." Elsewhere, hipster joints can feel like guilty compensation and are often populated by folks who dress in blue-collar duds to look like starving proletariats, but come sunrise, they earn six-figure salaries at Internet startups.

Fortunately, New Orleans hasn't played the trendy game in over a century. Rapid change just ain't our thing. Our city's climate makes jumping on fashion trends willy-nilly impossible if not dangerous. It's just too damn hot. Nor do we have an abundance of glitzy, high-tech startups or corporate parks. What we have is an abundance of people who don't make anywhere close to six figures and who have carved out unconventional and creative lives. And in a city smitten with its own traditions, our style may appear out of style, but we prefer it that way. New Orleans is a holdout city. Vintage is our substance.

That's not to say that New Orleans doesn't evolve, only that things change at their own pace. So what we call a hipster bar isn't exactly like the kind you'll find elsewhere in urban America— the kind that can be self-consciously cool and gimmicky. We don't have bars with all-white decor. In the French Quarter, where most buildings are over 150 years old, we just can't pull off brand-spanking new.

Nor do we want to. Instead, what our hipsters seek is a fresh take on an authentic look. New Orleans' hipster bars are a lot like dives that have been given a good mopping and a new coat of paint. Their patrons tend to be on the younger side, aware of trend but not beholden to it, and looking for drinks and decor that merge tradition with a modern cosmopolitan consciousness.

Name: Bar Tonique

Address: 820 North Rampart Street

Phone: 504-324-6045

Web site: www.BarTonique.com

Your tab: Slightly pricier than other bars in the area but still affordable. This is Rampart Street, after all.

What you're swilling: Bar Tonique runs drink specials every day of the week, from Pimm's cups to Caipirinhas. If you're a wine buff, you're in luck: Tonique's collections of reds, whites, rosés, sparkling wines, and ports are impressive—doubly so for what is, in effect, a nicely turned out neighborhood bar.

What you're wearing: Although Tonique is located on the downscale side of the Quarter, patrons here are happy to step up their sartorial game. Sure, you can show up in shorts and a T-shirt—this isn't one of those annoying, uppity "mixologist" joints (you know the kind we mean) that comes with a pain-in-the-butt dress code. However, you'll probably feel more in sync if you play the dapper card.

What you're hearing: The music rotation on the speaker varies, but the volume is always kept at a reasonable level, so you can sit and have a decent conversation—as you should, over cocktails, right?

Tattoo themes: Ink is on full display here. You may see a few Bettie Pages and a handful of traditional Japanese designs. But in our experience, the tats at Tonique are a little more original: quirky line drawings and odd icons symbolizing key moments in the owner's life.

Your drinking buddies: To call the Tonique crowd "hipsters" is a bit facile. Yes, that crowd's afoot, but given the bar's location, Tonique also draws everyday folks from the neighborhood and aficionados in search of a well-made drink.

Best feature: The banquettes around the edge of the room are great for people-watching, but our favorite feature is Bar Tonique's extensive menu of "Temperance Drinks" (aka non-alcoholic beverages)—a real rarity in the Quarter. You and your teetotalling pals can be just as festive and entertaining swilling pineapple phosphates as you can downing a slew of mai tais.

We love Rampart Street. It's just three blocks from Bourbon Street, but it feels miles away. There are people here, to be sure, but not the throngs you find elsewhere in the Quarter. On Rampart, locals and a few tourists travel in groups of two or three, often just passing through en route to someplace more lively.

But in our world, "lively" isn't always a draw. More often than not, we'd rather park it on a banquette in a quiet, neighborhood bar and catch up on the latest gossip while knocking back a few well-made drinks. And so, we've come to Bar Tonique. It's perfect for those in search of a good drink, away from most of the maddening crowd.

That said, we're not alone. In the far corner, someone's having a birthday celebration. It's not too rowdy but loud enough that we could gather enough information to blackmail most of those in attendance. There are a few people at the bar, too—mostly cute 20- and 30-somethings with zippy metabolisms that allow them to sit comfortably in skinny jeans.

This is our first stop of the night, so we're feeling a little indecisive. We ask the bartender to surprise us. She spins around, whips out a shaker, adds a series of ingredients, and does what looks to be an ancient cocktail-shaking dance. Bing, bang, boom, and the next thing we know, there are three full glasses on the bar in front of us.

"Thanks!" Richard says. "Um, what are they?" he asks, breaking Tippler Rule #1: looking a gift bartender in the mouth.

"Moscow mules. They're on special."

Perfect. The Moscow mule is a refreshing mix of vodka, ginger beer, and lime juice. It was a huge hit in the 1950s, but no one makes them much anymore—in part because few bars stock ginger beer. Bar Tonique doesn't either, but they get the gist of it by using their homemade ginger syrup and club soda.

Two rounds later, we're contemplating joining the birthday gang, but they saunter off to parts unknown before we can infiltrate the party. It's just as well; our perch is so comfortable and the banter so good that we've decided to skip the rest of our plans and park it here for the night. Like love and good pasta, when the bar vibe is right, you just know it.

Name: Meauxbar Bistro
Address: 942 North Rampart Street (at St. Philip Street)
Phone: 504-569-9979
Web site: www.MeauxBar.com
Your tab: Average. You'll pay more than you would at some Rampart Street joints, but this is a restaurant—and a good one at that. The wine list is strong, and some of the by-the-glass vintages are very reasonably priced.
What you're swilling: You could go for one of the restaurant's specialty drinks or a pleasant Côtes du Rhône, but why not go full-on French and order up a glass of bubbly?
What you're wearing: Something snappy. There's no dress code, so jeans are fine, but you might want to amp things up with a good jacket and a nice pair of shoes.
What you're hearing: There's canned music, but honestly, you're more likely to hear boozy conversations from some of the diners. We won't lie: it can get a little noisy.
Tattoo themes: Ink isn't on full display here. It's not hidden, mind you, but it takes a backseat.
Your drinking buddies: Locals (and the occasional tourist) out for a night on the town and a very good meal
Best feature: As charming as Meauxbar is, it's far more of a restaurant than a bar. Order up some small plates (try the steak tartare!), and don't forget dessert.

It's one of those nights in the French Quarter—one of those nights when the streets are packed, and parking is impossible to find. Ordinarily, we'd walk or ride our bikes, but tonight, we've come from a restaurant out by Lake Pontchartrain, and we're en route to a pre-pre-Bastille Day party in the middle of the Quarter. A car is a necessary evil.

After half an hour of circling, we find a spot, but it's far from where we need to be. Thankfully, we're one block from Meauxbar. What better place to grab a Francophile drink for the walk ahead than one of the neighborhood's best French bistros?

Entering through the curtain, we realize that we're not the only ones with this idea. The tables are packed, but thankfully, the bar is mostly empty. We slide up and order: three Pernods, please.

Ordinarily, that wouldn't be such a wise choice, since Pernod is on the strong side. But our bellies are full, and there's something about the taste of anisette that revives us from the wilting July heat. Halfway through our second drinks, though, we notice that we're not quite as full as we thought. To play it safe, we order a few things to nibble on. And just to be super-French (note: that is not technically a word), we include the steak tartare. It is possibly one of the most heavenly things we have ever consumed in the history of ever. We make a note of it for future reference.

By the time we finally toddle out, we've nixed our plans for the pre-pre-Bastille Day party. We're not drunk, but the thought of hanging out at a bar and celebrating the French Revolution when we've just had one of the most French drinking (and eating) experiences the Quarter can offer seems anticlimactic. Never let it be said that we don't know when to say when.

Name: One Eyed Jacks/The Matador
Address: 615 Toulouse Street
Phone: 504-569-8361, but seriously, don't bother.
Web site: www.OneEyedJacks.net
Your tab: Cheap. Jacks is generally cash only, but ask nicely and they'll ring cards at the front bar.
What you're swilling: High Life and PBR are on permanent special, but Jack and Coke is popular, too. If Candace is around, be sure to ask for a couple of her "specialty shots," just for good measure.
What you're wearing: Jeans, flip-flops, and threadbare T-shirts or skinny-pants/emo ensembles for guys. Girls sport cute alt-wear, including bustiers and really good boots. Wigs get you bonus points.
What you're hearing: Blondie, David Bowie (pre-"China Girl"), T. Rex, Foreigner, and Duran Duran on the speaker—basically anything with a guitar that hasn't been playing on Clear Channel stations. Aside from Thursday '80s nights, the club does host shows and mostly caters to alt-rock groups, usually with local warm-up bands. See the Web site for their lineup.
Tattoo themes: Any and all, though Bettie Page is awfully popular.
Your drinking buddies: Everyone in New Orleans: Quarter residents, suburbanites, college kids, gays who've wandered over from the Fruit Loop, tourists, and plenty of downtowners. Amazingly, everyone gets along just fine
Best feature: Apart from the antique chandelier in the front bar and all the black-velvet Elvises and naked ladies on the walls, we're smitten by the semisecret bar upstairs called the Matador. You may have to ask the bartender how to find the half-hidden door—which, of course, is part of the fun. (Note: the front bar is always available for drinking, and unlike the back bar, which charges a cover for shows, the front is always free except on '80s Night.)

Photograph by John d'Addario

All roads lead to One Eyed Jacks—at least it seems so on Thursday '80s Night. Despite the fact that it's late July (low season), hours after sunset but still 90 degrees, and not quite the weekend, much of the modern world has gathered on Toulouse Street to swill two-dollar High Lifes and one-dollar PBRs and sway to Depeche Mode on the speaker.

It's 11:00 P.M. when Elizabeth and Richard settle onto the pleather banquette across from the bar. Allison calls to say she's running late, and for a good half-hour, the pair are content to sit under a buxom, copper-haired nude on velvet and people-watch. A small herd of Microsoft conventioneers wearing Windows T-shirts is gradually being edged out by hipsters, pretty boys, and what appear to be three generations of a clan from New Zealand. And when we grow tired of perusing the people, we enjoy looking at the bar itself. Most establishments in the Quarter claim to have once been houses of ill repute, but in the half-light of a dusty chandelier, One Eyed Jacks' origins seem less apocryphal than most. It's a bar that understands what we want from the Big Queasy—gilt mirrors and flocked wallpaper that feed our inner madam.

Outside, Allison finally takes her place in line, which stretches down the block. It's an 18-and-up event, and even though most of the crowd can't have been alive for more than three hours of the 1980s, it seems that half of underage suburbia has found their way here. What exactly the 1980s—the last full decade of the Cold War—mean to the youth of the Digital Age isn't clear; Allison notes with disappointment that she's the only one sporting a *Flashdance* shoulder peep. However, what is abundantly clear is that '80s Night is a coming-of-age ritual for the subdivision set.

"I don't see why I have to show an ID at all," complains a brunette with defiantly flat-ironed hair. "I mean, I am 20."

Elizabeth and Richard make room for Allison on the bench. By now, the front bar is forested with bodies, but our favorite patron clomps in after midnight: Transformer Man! Really— he's wearing an assortment of cardboard boxes, taped together.

New Orleanians don't blink. Microsoft does. They probably don't get this in Redmond. Halloween is months off and Mardi Gras farther still, but it's always open season for costuming in this town. The crowd parts to let Transformer Man pass, and he galumphs his way towards the dancehall, struggling on the stairs. We suspect it's not Transformer's first '80s Night. The homemade costume shows some obvious wear. Still, when we think of how hot it must be under all those cardboard boxes, it's hard not to see him as a small gift to the world.

When Richard announces he has to get up early, Allison promptly orders another round. Twenty minutes later, Richard takes the remainder of his brew in a go-cup to keep him company on the walk home.

We fight our way into the pulsing beats of the back room. The dancehall is much larger than the lobby, but even so, it's packed. Inside the circular bar, two women mix drinks with the focused precision of gladiators. There's no hope of getting a round of cocktails in here, so we make our way to the front of the dance floor and carve out a patch of boogie turf. Entranced by our historic moves, a lanky pair of underage boys moves in. And then, a beautiful thing happens. The DJ offers up four courses of 1980s perfection: "Melt with You," "Lose Your Love Tonight," "My Sharona," and "Video Killed the Radio Star." The Toni Home Perm kinks its way back into our hair.

Then, the first pings of "Take On Me" chirp out, and it's over as soon as it began.

"Oh, this is *A*-ha," one of our new protégés says.

"A-*ha,*" Elizabeth gently corrects.

We maneuver back towards the lobby bar. Reason would dictate heading home. It's past two. And it's Thursday. We settle on a nightcap—upstairs at the bar within the bar, the Matador.

Open only when the crowd is expected to be large, the Matador is the third and final level of One Eyed Jacks. The Matador is a semisecret space, a refuge from the Proactiv hordes below. Word to the wise: if you didn't know this bar was here, you'd never find it—the door blends in with the wall of the lobby bar. Of course, the fact that not everyone is meant to find the Matador makes it all the more desirable. Here you can find a seat. Here there is no wait for a drink. Here the velvet paintings are of bulls. We heart the Matador. It's dark and red and intimate. If you are a woman, you feel like Sophia Loren; if you are a man, you feel like Steve McQueen. Here you are an international lover, a spy. Here you are the inspiration for one of the velvet nudes downstairs. But you won't say which, because like the Matador, you have secrets.

Here, lifting your glass is an act of seduction. Here you can make anyone fall in love with you. It's now 3:00 A.M., and we have fallen hopelessly for ourselves.

Name: St. Lawrence
Address: 219 North Peters Street
Phone: 504-525-4111
Web site: www.saintlawrencenola.com
Your tab: Varies. Cocktails can be a bit pricey, though regular call drinks and beer won't set you too far back.
What you're swilling: Nice cocktails and the freshly made daiquiris
What you're wearing: Whatever you've been walking around the Quarter in
What you're hearing: Hipster soundtrack on the speaker
When you're there: For late-night munchies or a midday drink
Tattoo themes: No constant themes, though Caleb, the ginger-haired chef, sports some pretty interesting ink
Your drinking buddies: The repurposed daiquiri machines
Best feature: Freshly made juice-based frozen daiquiris

New Orleans is a Catholic town. Cashiers at local grocery stores such as Dorignac's and Langenstein's wear smocks covered with pins of the Blessed Mother and St. Francis. Ask the shoppers in line with you for a lucky St. Joseph bean, and you should easily collect a dozen or more. Make your groceries on Ash Wednesday, and everyone walking the aisles looks as if they just cleaned out their charcoal grill. Even our football team is the Saints. So it's about time that someone launched a venue named after St. Lawrence, the patron saint of chefs.

St. Lawrence is the product of Caleb Cook, a former chef at Mondo, part of the Susan Spicer empire, so we walk in knowing that his food will have chops. The surprise in the bar comes from its clever take on a New Orleans standard drink.

The space feels as though the owners had 48 hours to turn an empty place into a bar. Its decor is hip minimalism but not in a pretentious, expensive way. The bar itself looks as if it is constructed from repurposed cabinets, and bead board covers much of the ductwork on the exposed ceiling.

St. Lawrence fits into the new category of hipster restaurant, one that offers a quality cocktail list featuring twists on classics (a Sazerac made with rum) as well as at least one drink with St. Germain, the ketchup of bartenders. But the *pièce de résistance* is what is proffered from the daiquiri machines. The previous restaurant owners left them as part of the turnkey package and Caleb and the rest of the staff decided to incorporate them into their cocktail menu, but they start with fresh juice instead of the traditional artificial base. The frozen Pimm's cup is now a permanent flavor, but tonight we rave over the slushy Muscadine sangria. Our locally based treats wash down similarly themed Louisiana fare: juicy turducken burgers.

We finish our daiquiris and head out to meet friends. As we do, we notice that the electrical box by the door has been turned into a small altar. We briefly genuflect to St. Lawrence, grateful for a quality frozen drink.

Name: SoBou

Address: 310 Chartres Street

Phone: 504-552-4095

Web site: www.sobounola.com

Your tab: Pricey, though worth it

What you're swilling: Craft cocktails, beer

What you're wearing: Ideally, some nice togs. The place did get listed as one of the best new restaurants in the U.S.

What you're hearing: Lots of chatter. Even on a weeknight, the bar is full.

Tattoo themes: Discreetly hidden

Your drinking buddies: Hotel guests, hipsters, stylish singles

Best feature: The creative cocktail menu, though the ice block is a prominent detail

New Orleans knows who she is. The city's neighborhoods—Uptown, Downtown, and Mid-City—were labeled long ago in terms of their relation to water, specifically the Mississippi River and Lake Pontchartrain. The curves of the river make cardinal directions pretty useless here unless you have a compass handy. Instead, we give our directions in terms of the "lakeside" or "riverside" and "downtown" or "uptown" side of the street. Even the city's permits specify that work be completed, for example, "on lakeside and uptown side" of a French Quarter building.

So we had a grumpy response to SoBou, which stands for "South of Bourbon." The name is a direct nod to New York's SoHo, Nolita, and TriBeCa, though other cities have picked up the trend, such as San Francisco's SoMa and Austin's SoCo. Prior to this bar opening, we had no idea it was south of Bourbon, just closer to the river.

We guess a name like this is to be expected for a bar set in the W, a boutique hotel geared to a trendy crowd. But happily, the name was the only disappointment of the evening.

We visit SoBou on a lively Friday evening. The design of the space is as hip and modern as its name. Its exposed beams and brick lend a sleek and cool air. An IKEA-inspired wire-mesh shelf floats above, holding most of the glassware. The sleek granite bar houses a backlit glass square on one end that gives off a soft radiance, a modern version of candlelight in which everyone glows. The bar is packed, as are the tables nearby, which have beer taps placed in the middle of them. Apparently, the taps measure themselves; you can sit and drink beer all evening with no need to refill your mug at the bar.

We worry that the service might be a little stuffy, as is often the case when your drinks are "crafted" by a "mixologist," but bartender Abigail is friendly and helpful, explaining ingredients and offering suggestions, even on this busy night. Allison enjoys a traditional daiquiri, Elizabeth chooses a riff on a Sazerac, and Richard samples the punch. Bartenders periodically chip large cubes from an enormous ice block, chilling the several dozens of rums, bourbons, and scotches available. Quarts of the Bitter Truth bitters are lined up, ready to refill the smaller bottles the bartenders use, and our friend Karen notes that Unicum, a rare Hungarian digestif liqueur, is also for sale.

SoBou is relatively new on the social scene and a destination for the city's Bright Young Things. Two young women whose tans are only slightly more golden than their perfectly ironed hair flirt effortlessly with the young well-groomed bucks on adjacent barstools. After an abundance of hair tossing and one smoldering over-the-shoulder glance, the ladies leave for their dinner table, the promise of meeting up later for drinks lingering in the air. We're just happy they leave empty barstools. We settle in to drink in comfort, and talk returns to the bar's name. Our delicious drinks make us feel more benevolently towards the Big Apple's influence on our French Quarter. New Orleans has welcomed traditions from around the globe. We decide that maybe the city has room for a nod to Gotham City after all.

Photograph by John d'Addario

Name: Sylvain
Address: 625 Chartres Street
Phone: 504-265-8123
Web site: www.sylvain.com
Your tab: $3-90 per drink, excluding tip
What you're swilling: You make the call.
What you're wearing: Euro casual
What you're hearing: Rock and roll, new and old, on the speaker
When you're there: Like the mints, after eight
Tattoo themes: Understated
Your drinking buddies: Dates, friends, hip relations, forward-thinking colleagues
Best feature: Tasteful decor

By New Orleans standards, Sylvain hasn't been open for business long. However, the gastro pub, located in a prime spot just a few steps from Jackson Square, already has the look of something that could have been around for years. In a way, it has. Though the design includes considered, charcoal, TV-less walls, Sylvain hasn't been so redone that it's lost its links to the past. The original French doors and beamed ceilings still define the space. Sylvain feels slim and effortlessly chic. Even the alleyway tables flanking the rear-building kitchen and the narrow courtyard beyond exude an easy style that falls short of precious. Like a great jacket, Sylvain offers the kind of lines that make everyone within them appear slightly more attractive and intelligent.

The Tipplers gather around one of the smooth tabletops crafted from yellow pine, a nod to the same wood found on the floors of every shotgun cottage in the city. We could choose from the cocktails that run about $10 apiece, wine by the glass at about $12, or, for $5, the homegrown and hoppy LA 31 IPA on draft. Some would hesitate to call Sylvain a bar; in truth, it's not. It's known for its Southern pub fare and slightly upscale takes on pulled pork and fried chicken sandwiches. But tonight the Tipplers don't care about maintaining strict boundaries. We only care about what we like.

After all, New Orleans has always been willingn to transcend categories. Poised between tradition and reinvention, the city reveals this kinda-sorta quality in many ways, such as the fact that New Orleanians claim we're not *really* a part of the United States, despite what the maps might indicate. We mean that our city sometimes harbors a Caribbean essence, sometimes European, sometimes even Third World. The Quarter can feel especially reluctant to admit it belongs to the United States. Indeed, if it weren't for the framed heirloom Stars and Stripes on Sylvain's wall, it would be easy to forget that we were still in America. It's the kind of blurring that can drive Type As into aneurysms before they move away.

Like the Quarter, Sylvain draws from numerous sources: British and French at first glance, but also Southern on closer inspection. This is probably the only place in the Quarter where you can pair crushed field peas on toast with a $3 can of Schlitz, and as far as the Tipplers can say, it *is the* only entry to present a bottle of Veuve Cliquot with hand-cut fries ($90) as an appetizer.

The music seamlessly moves between Fleetwood Mac and Oasis, low enough not to compete with conversation. Without the distraction of a flickering screen or a football game, that's what most of the patrons in Sylvain are doing, just talking. And sure enough after nine, when the emphasis shifts from dinner to drinking, we feel extra justified in keeping Sylvain on our list of 100 bars. The dozen or so stools along the bar fill, while a few drinkers stand. It's a mixed crowd: locals, discreet tourists, couples, friends, and solos in for a pint or glass of wine and the latest copy of the *Gambit Weekly* for company.

On the wall behind us is a print of Ben Franklin, looking so very much like himself, standing at the center of the French court. He's attempting to convince the soon-to-be beheaded of the value of the American colonial cause. The date reads 1776;

the Vieux Carré wasn't American or French, and we're reminded that New Orleans wasn't a part of either revolution.

Nevertheless, the Tipplers raise a glass to Franklin. Though he is known for his calendars and lists, his legacy is quintessentially like New Orleans': one that defies category. He was a pacifist, writer, brewer, believer in the value of alehouse debate, journalist, deft kite handler, and, despite all appearances, *lover*, perhaps of some of the very culotted *dames* pictured over the Tipplers' gratefully intact heads. We're pretty sure that, if given the chance, Franklin would have had a good time at Sylvain.

CHAPTER 9

Hotel Bars

Let's start with a small apology. This chapter can be confusing because by now, you've read other chapters with bars housed in hotels. While the Sazerac and Carousel Bar are indeed hotel bars, these elegant mainstays are often frequented by locals and visitors who will never sleep upstairs, and we felt they deserved iconic status. And there are other bars rooted in hotels, such as hip SoBou or Irvin Mayfield's Jazz Playhouse. These, too, we felt were better fits for other categories.

But there's another kind of hotel bar that deserves mention. While not generally where the locals go and in fact unknown to many locals, these bars are less upscale than the ones listed above. The establishments included in this chapter are the kind that don't require dressing up. You can even wear pajamas or a cover-up between dips in the pool.

Generally, these hotel bars are low-key, decompression zones where you can take a seat each night and pump the bartender for dinner suggestions. Comfortable, clean, casual, and often discreet, these spots are deliberately designed not to push boundaries or offend anyone's tastes. The places listed here keep hotel patrons and the occasional passerby well watered. If your hotel or bed and breakfast doesn't have a bar, let any on this list be your stand-in.

Name: Bistreaux at Le Meritage
Address: 1001 Toulouse Street (Maison Dupuy Hotel)
Phone: 504-522-8800
Web site: www.lemeritagerestaurant.com/bistreaux-menu.html
Your tab: $8-10 for glass of wine or specialty cocktail; $5 for quality beer
What you're swilling: Malbec, Stella Artois, Guinness
What you're wearing: Corporate casual
What you're hearing: Very little
When you're there: For a nightcap or before heading out
Tattoo themes: Hidden
Your drinking buddies: Tourists, hotel guests
Best feature: Tie between the quiet and the courtyard

So it's now official. Whenever possible, Louisianians must replace *o* with *eaux: Geaux, Tigers; Meauxbar; Preaux Life* (we're not kidding). And so we arrive at the inevitable, *bistreaux.*

Despite its corner location, the Bistreaux at Le Meritage is on the edge of the Quarter and rarely crowded. It's an offshoot of the decidedly more upscale Meritage restaurant on the other side of the wall, both of which are located in the sizable Maison Dupuy Hotel. We know, it's a lot of names to remember.

From the outside, the Bistreaux may also seem too upscale for the quantity-driven drinker. Indeed, this isn't the place for a cheap well drink or a two-dollar Miller High Life, but decent beer and wine prices are in keeping with the rest of the Quarter. What isn't in keeping with the rest of the Quarter is the feel of the place. The Bistreaux isn't bohemian or historic or divey or glam or neighborhoody like Fahy's across the street. Instead there's a dark, slightly corporate, *Lost in Translation* feel to the space that's only reinforced by the Toulouse-Lautrec-esque murals on the walls and the universal wood paneling. In short, it's a hotel bar. But unlike some other hotel bars in the Quarter, the Bistreaux *feels* like a hotel bar.

For the record, tipplers can take their drinks into the spacious landscaped courtyard, with its pool and Versailles-worthy cupid fountain, and experience a different vibe altogether. But back inside, we Tipplers understand that there's a time and place for every mood. Needs can change rapidly in the Quarter. Not everyone is up for the sensation overload of Bourbon Street or the gut gymnastics of cheap vodka. And after three or four hours, even the highest-flying *geaux*, *geaux*, *geaux* types can find themselves crashing and burning. So at those moments, a little darkness and background music; some unchallenging but tasteful, smoke-free decor; and a professional-looking bartender (not to mention the possibility of ordering cheddar and scallion fries from the bar menu) may make the emergency landing a little less painful.

Name: The Burgundy Bar
Address: 931 Canal Street (The Saint)
Phone: 504-522-5400
Web site: www.TheSaintHotelNewOrleans.com
Your tab: It's a hotel bar, so prices are naturally a little higher. Plan accordingly.
What you're swilling: The bar is well stocked, so you're welcome to knock back anything you like. However, it might be best to keep things simple. (See the review below.)
What you're wearing: The decor is fairly upscale, and you can go that route if you like, but we've spotted people wearing Tommy Bahama at the bar. Translation: anything goes.
What you're hearing: Like some other hotel boîtes, the Burgundy Bar offers a rotating series of live jazz performances.
Tattoo themes: The Saint is a relatively new, hip hotel, aimed at youngish travelers looking for something edgier than your average Holiday Inn experience, which means that there's plenty of ink to go around.
Your drinking buddies: Mostly tourists stopping in for a drink before heading out for the night. Many locals haven't found it yet, but that's slowly changing.
Best feature: It's pretty. And the live jazz doesn't hurt either.

Walking into the Saint, we're a little taken aback. The lobby and adjoining restaurant are overwrought, like an evening gown made by a fashion designer who's just graduated from college. There's too much going on.

We veer to the left, into the Burgundy Bar, and the situation immediately improves. The low lighting and the sounds of live jazz make it feel more intimate and special. Elizabeth and Allison order martinis to match the swanky vibe.

Then, things go off the rails. Richard's gotten a head-start on his drinking and wants to slow down the pace. So he asks the woman behind the bar for his go-to booze-free beverage: a bitters and soda.

The bartender blinks once, twice, three times. "Bourbon and soda?"

"Bitters, please."

"I don't think we have that."

Richard patiently walks a few feet down the bar and points at a small, brown bottle. "Bitters. Angostura, if you have it."

The bartender picks up the bottle and holds it up to the light. Maybe she's never noticed it before. Or maybe she's wondering if Barbara Eden is asleep inside.

Eventually, she fills a tumbler with ice and soda, opens the bottle of bitters, and goes to pour it in. Except, of course, you don't pour bitters, you splash it. She is very, very confused.

"Just use about five splashes," Richard suggests. She does this, then hands it to him. "Could I get that with a twist of lemon?" She begrudgingly obliges, making him the simplest cocktail in the world.

Apart from that very strange glitch, the rest of our visit goes smoothly. The tide of patrons—mostly hotel guests by the look of it—ebbs and flows, but the jazz band keeps playing. If we were out-of-towners, this would be a great place to start the night, provided we were all drinking martinis.

Name: The Green Bar
Address: 100 Iberville Street (in the Westin Hotel)
Phone: 504-553-5140
Your tab: $10-12 for a specialty cocktail; $6 for a draft beer
What you're swilling: A considered cocktail menu changes seasonally: mojitos for hot times; heartier, browner liqueurs for "fall" and "winter"—or New Orleans' versions of these seasons.
What you're wearing: Corporate casual or European shorts and mandals for guys; jeans and up for the ladies
What you're hearing: Locals Dr. John or Trombone Shorty or classics like Etta James and Ella Fitzgerald on the speaker
When you're there: Afternoon and early evening for the best view from the hotel lobby
Tattoo themes: Few and far between
Your drinking buddies: Hotel guests
Best feature: View of the mighty Mississippi and the Quarter from the hotel lobby

Not surprisingly, the Green Bar's drinks are on the pricey side but, to their credit, stiff. We and our guest Tipplers order old fashioneds and Abitas, and Richard says to follow him down the hall; the reason to drink in the Westin, he tells us, is the lobby. There's nothing wrong with the Green Bar per se, but it's windowless, a bit closed off, and a little on the slick, corporate side.

As we enter the lobby, the space suddenly opens up and we all breathe out. With its stretches of marble tile and high box-beamed ceiling, it evokes a bit of *The Great Gatsby*. Of all the bars the Tipplers have covered in our yearlong swill junket, the Westin offers the most expansive space. And it's here that we're reminded that the Westin is located on the top floors of a modern, midrise building, unconstrained by the 12-foot-wide shotgun proportions that those who frequent the Quarter come to expect. Indeed, there's really nothing in this decidedly 20th-century lobby to link it to typical Quarter architecture—no cracked plaster walls or French doors opening onto a sidewalk, no patina/crust of age or smell of humanity. In comparison, the Westin's lobby feels like the size of a football field.

We arrange ourselves in one of the sofas-and-velveteen-club-chair seatings (upholstery!) and instantly recognize that we'll be here a while. Because even more than the space *inside*, the Westin affords a sense of the space *outside*. Through the span of picture windows, we see the pink and terracotta-colored townhouses lining Decatur Street as well as the river itself. Despite living in the city since 2003, Elizabeth and Allison have never seen this view. In turn, we rise from our seats and press our fingers on the glass.

It may seem strange to most visitors, but outside of hurricane season, it can be easy for locals to *forget* about the Mississippi River. The Quarter is particularly walled off from the water. The world's fourth-longest river flows just beyond Café Du Monde, but usually we don't get farther than the beignets. Of course, the Mississippi is our city's raison d'être and one of the official borders of the Vieux Carré, but we don't see it unless we make the effort. And it can be the same for the Quarter itself. The very reason we love it—the intimacy of its human proportions—also means that we rarely get a bird's-eye view of the neighborhood. As anyone who lives here soon discovers, our city is not one of vistas. The Quarter looks *into* itself, not without.

Richard says he comes to this lobby from time to time. It's like taking a vacation within his own city, affording a change of perspective and a place to stretch out and cool down. And though the Tipplers already have plenty of reasons to like drinking, this reason is certainly among them. For the cost of a single cocktail, one can inhabit a different space for a half-hour or, if really nursed, an hour. With that in mind, $10 seems like a bargain.

Name: May Baily's Place
Address: 415 Dauphine Street (Dauphine Orleans Hotel)
Phone: 504-588-1314
Web site: www.dauphineorleans.com/nightlife
Your tab: Moderate
What you're swilling: This is a good bar to get a classic cocktail such as a rusty nail or old fashioned.
What you're wearing: Tank top and shorts are okay.
What you're hearing: A little jazz on the speaker, or the TV if a Saints game is on
Tattoo themes: None
Your drinking buddies: Fellow hotel guests, a smattering of locals
Best feature: The Storyville paraphernalia

The upper blocks of Bourbon Street (near Canal Street) are a veritable buffet of flesh, with strip clubs flanking both sides of the street. We're a port town, folks, and historically have offered visitors a heady mixture of sex and booze with some good music and food thrown in as lagniappe. One brothel was located where the bar May Baily's sits today, named in honor of the original madam and owner.

We order an old fashioned, rusty nail, and sidecar, which are spot on—not too sweet and plenty strong—then explore the bar. Visitors to nearby Storyville, the 16-block headquarters of Big Easy fleshpots from 1897 to 1917, relied upon the *New Orleans Blue Book*, an index of prostitutes and the locales where they plied their trade. May Baily's walls bear framed excerpts from that list. As we circle around the bar, we read about the Oriental Danseuse, Prettie Sadie Reed, and Annie Ross, "The Queen of Smile." Images of the "ladies of the night" captured by local photographer E. J. Bellocq dot the walls as well. A framed newspaper page from the 1830s bears the title *Sporting News* and recounts the zesty and licentious behavior of the city. The *pièce de résistance* of memorabilia is the brothel license awarded in 1858 to May Baily, signed by the mayor.

We imagine the room lit only with gas, the few patrons at the bar now a different kind of clientele. Though we objectively know that working in a brothel was a hard life, images from *Pretty Baby* and *The Best Little Whorehouse in Texas* collide in our minds, and we see ourselves clad only in our skivvies, sipping whiskey while shimmying to this new music called jazz.

We have been told the hotel's courtyard is charming, so we move outside. Blessed and longed-for autumn has finally arrived, and Elizabeth eagerly pulls a sweater from her bag, the first long sleeves of the fall. The hotel's pool dominates the space, and tonight the few tables scattered around it are empty: we have the courtyard to ourselves. The soft swish of the water lapping against the pool walls is the only sound, but we imagine the strains of a piano coming from inside, with some player pounding out a Joplin rag.

Name: Vacherie

Address: 827 Toulouse Street (Hotel St. Marie)

Phone: 504-207-4532

Web site: www.vacherierestaurant.com

Your tab: Moderate

What you're swilling: Whatever floats your boat; decent cocktails and beers

What you're wearing: Your most iconic "tourist" outfit

What you're hearing: A little TV, though chatting with the bartender is nicer.

Tattoo themes: None

Your drinking buddies: Whoever you are visiting New Orleans with

Best feature: Camaraderie

We pop into Vacherie one evening to get a walking-around drink. Their prices are reasonable, and their bathroom is spotless, so we decide to make a pit stop en route to meeting friends across the Quarter. In the 10 minutes we are there, we experience the diverse crowd that pours through a hotel bar's turnstiles:

Well-togged arrivals to a wedding rehearsal dinner sip on pre-dinner cocktails.

San Diego Chargers fans, in for the Saints game, nurse bloody marys.

Two pedicab drivers order postshift draft beers.

A hotel guest, still dripping from the pool, gets his vodka and soda to go.

With the exception of the dinner guests, all greet bartender Victoria by name. We expect this of the pedicab drivers, who are clearly local, but are surprised by the rest. Victoria, who used to work at a local bar in the Central Business District, notes that she now has a different kind of regular: the hotel guest who starts his night in the bar before dinner, or stops here before heading to bed, or even orders an eye-opener post-breakfast. Her regulars don't stick around as long here, but she feels as though she gets to know them with the same kind of intimacy. "People are always looking for that neighborhood experience. They like knowing my name and when I know theirs. Even on vacation, you want to feel like you are home."

We gather our drinks and head out, leaving everyone to their own version of a local bar, even if it's only for the night.

CHAPTER 10

Other Bars

While we were compiling our 100, we realized that some bars didn't quite fit the categories we'd created. They weren't neighborhood or hipster or highbrow. Like New Orleans itself, some bars defy labels. That doesn't make them any less satisfying or worthwhile, and in some cases, that difference has allowed places to fill a niche.

A couple of the bars, namely Cafe Pontalba and Pirate's Alley Café, are here because of their charming locations within the Quarter. But most of the bars that follow are housed in restaurants, and if the Tipplers love anything more than drinking, it's eating *and* drinking. Since these are places that don't require reservations, if the atmosphere is a fit for you, drinks can effortlessly segue into dinner. And if you want to get a burger at the perennial favorite Port of Call, there's always a line, so you might as well wait out the hour with a drink. That said, these establishments have established bars, and you can feel comfortable entering and not ordering food.

Our final entries, Sidney's Wine Cellar and Vieux Carré Wine and Spirits, are really stores but Vieux Carré allows drinking on the premises, and both offer the opportunity to bring the bar back home. We feel that it's a fitting end to our tour or, perhaps, the chance to start all over again.

Name: Cafe Pontalba
Address: 546 St. Peter Street
Phone: 504-522-1180
Your tab: Very reasonable if you stick with the standards
What you're swilling: Booze and mixer or a beer
What you're wearing: Oh, just come as you are. Everyone else did.
What you're hearing: Lots of folks talking about the beignets they had that morning or the number of hurricanes they downed last night—though not everyone here is a tourist. Try to drown them out and enjoy the view.
Tattoo themes: It completely depends on the time of year and which conventions are in town. Cafe Pontalba isn't an especially local joint, though, so fleurs-de-lis will be few and far between (except on the staff and the French Quarter workers who've stopped by for a drink on their way home).
Your drinking buddies: Though there are some service-industry types afoot, a great number of drinkers at the Cafe Pontalba have never been here before. Make friends with your fellow travelers.
Best feature: The view of Jackson Square

When out-of-town friends and family arrive on our doorstep, stop number one for them is the French Quarter. We locals often hold firm about which "tourist traps" are to be avoided at all costs, steering them to the "cool spots" instead. Surprisingly, some of these more touristy venues offer as authentic an experience as the hippest tavern.

Cafe Pontalba sits just across from St. Louis Cathedral, housed at the corner of one set of the Pontalba apartments, some of the oldest apartments in the United States. The city of New Orleans and state of Louisiana each own a building, so they remain very high end rental properties. Living in one comes with a certain cachet, since political connections are usually required. The closest many will ever get to hanging out in a Pontalba apartment is having a drink at this bar.

The restaurant's long marble bar faces a lovely mirrored back bar that evokes its 19th-century roots. We order from Frank, the weekend bartender, and soon sip large drinks at tiny prices. Elizabeth's five-dollar gin and tonic is a generous 12-ounce pour, and Richard's Abita is four dollars. All the drinkers along the bar are locals who live and work in the Quarter. Frank tells us while many of his patrons are tourists, he gets lots of locals who come here because the drinks are strong and cheap, and the view is lovely. We turn in our stools to take in Jackson Square. The sun has begun to set, and the cathedral glows a dim, lovely gray. It is eminently satisfying to drink ardent spirits in view of a church, especially one that tolerates tippling as much as the Catholics do.

Europeans live with this ever-present reminder of the past, but most Americans do not. Spend time in the Quarter, and you constantly collide with history. The buildings are not a theme park created to lure visitors here but were constructed long ago for people to live and worship in. It doesn't take much to settle into that time. Frank serves our drinks in heavy glass tumblers instead of flimsy plastic cups. We turn away from the T-shirt-clad visitors and instead gaze on the majestic cathedral as we sway slightly to the sounds of a brass band playing the same tune heard here over 100 years ago.

Name: Café Soulé
Address: 720 St. Louis Street
Phone: 504-304-4636
Web site: www.cafesoule.com
Your tab: $8-11 per glass of wine or specialty cocktail; $5 per quality beer
What you're swilling: A glass of red wine or a classic New Orleans cocktail, such as a French 75, Sazerac, or New Orleans buck. Come morning, a bloody mary.
What you're wearing: Something casual but tasteful
What you're hearing: Background music on the speaker so soft you may not hear it
When you're there: Sunday-Thursday 7:30 A.M.-10:00 P.M.; Friday-Saturday till midnight
Tattoo themes: Flowers and vines
Your drinking buddies: Tourists but also a few locals
Best feature: Original architecture

The current rage in New Orleans is to name restaurants and bars after their original owners, usually men from the ranks of the city's early elite. So it is with Café Soulé, named after Pierre Soulé, a French nobleman whose political differences with Charles X caused Soulé to flee to New Orleans. After marrying a French Quarter belle, Soulé built a four-story mansion in 1830 and became Louisiana's first U.S. senator. Over a century later, the controversial politics of the building's inhabitants continued when New Orleans District Attorney Jim Garrison rented the third floor during his investigation into the assassination of Pres. John F. Kennedy and Garrison's unsuccessful attempt to prosecute local businessman Clay Shaw for the alleged conspiracy. From 2002 to 2008, the Soulé mansion was once again connected to the head of state when Gennifer Flowers, who claimed to have had a sexual relationship with former president Bill Clinton, owned the building.

However, none of Café Soulé's past intrigues are apparent

in its current incarnation as a simple French-based restaurant and bar. Café Soulé isn't for those seeking thrills, only tasteful surroundings. What now shines through are the original lines and spare, elegant proportions of what must have been the Soulés' front parlor. The current owners, who purchased the building in 2011, have dedicated themselves to restoring the original architecture. Even in a city of giants, the ceilings soar and have been painted a serene pale blue. Two sets of almost painfully pretty arched doors open onto St. Louis Street and look directly across to the Hermes Bar. French flags, a chandelier, an original mantel, and wood floors complete what is hard to find in the Quarter—a look that verges on understated.

And with only one flat-screen (among a record low for the Quarter), Café Soulé is all about low-level stimulation: conversation and drink and the pleasure of a space that's still a belle in the full light of day. Cocktails are pricey, but Soulé calls itself a craft bar. Tipplers can expect shaved ice and proper glasses, and if customers ask, the bartenders will concoct something using one of the colorful house-made simple syrups arrayed along the marble-topped bar. Café Soulé serves entrees and sandwiches for breakfast, lunch, and dinner, but the tippler's best bet is a sweet crepe and prosecco.

Or for those resilient enough to be standing come morning, Café Soulé may be the place to finally say goodbye to the night before with a bloody mary.

Name: Claire's Pour House
Address: 233 Decatur Street
Phone: 504-558-8980
Your tab: $2.50-$5 per drink
What you're swilling: $2.50 PBRs on draft; Tin Roof Pale Ale; simple cocktails
What you're wearing: Jeggings, a hoodie, and an iPod
What you're hearing: AC/DC, Billy Idol on the speaker
When you're there: After dark, when it's easier to see your iPhone screen
Tattoo themes: Boho, colorful
Your drinking buddies: Women's studies majors
Best feature: It's female centric.

It's Thursday, 9:00 P.M., when the Tipplers enter Claire's Pour House. Four young—as in AP-American history-looking-young—women, each with a gorgeous face and long hair, sit smoking at the bar and texting. At one point it seems as though they must be texting each other, as they simultaneously turn their stools towards each other, flash their glowing screens, and LOL.

The Tipplers take a row of stools at the very, very long wooden bar and spot something you don't see very often in the Quarter: small hooks underneath for hanging purses and lit so you can see while digging out a wallet or keys. And while Claire's is technically a dive (concrete floors, dim lighting, no floor-to-ceiling decorating scheme, no mixologist drink list), it's really too clean to be one. And despite the smoking, it's odor free. In the weeks before Halloween, strings of little ghosties hang from overhead. Perhaps you're getting the picture. If *Pretty in Pink* were a bar in the digital age, Claire's is it.

The bartender, an extremely polite and well groomed young man whose sexuality means that he will not be hitting on the clientele, confirms that in Claire's, estrogen reigns. He says that Claire herself is usually at the bar, and indeed most of the patrons are women and locals—a rarity for Decatur Street on both counts. In truth, it feels like a nice break. Even though the Tipplers have never felt threatened in a bar, drinking is still generally a man's game, and wherever men congregate, things can get loud and aggressive. In the Quarter, testosterone dominates. So does the male gaze—no matter at which gender it's directed. Female drinkers may put themselves in that kind of environment intentionally, but other times they end up there by default. It's good to know that Claire's offers an alternative, the kind of environment where a lone woman traveler can regroup or where local ladies can easily find themselves drawn into OMG-level conversations with their BFFs.

Name: Coyote Ugly

Address: 225 North Peters Street

Phone: 504-561-0003

Web site: www.CoyoteUglySaloon.com/NewOrleans

Your tab: Not too bad, until you start doing body shots. And you know you're going to start doing body shots.

What you're swilling: You can try to stick with beer, but the tequila's going to find its way down your throat before the night is through.

What you're wearing: Cargo shorts, Aéropostale, A&F, Ed Hardy, and flip-flops. Seriously, would you come here in a tie?

What you're hearing: Loud things on the speaker that you can probably sing along with

Tattoo themes: Flowers, cuffs around biceps and ankles, fraternity letters, and other things that people regretted a week after the scabs were gone

Your drinking buddies: The young, the desperate, and those with nothing better to do. Mostly tourists. Is this surprising?

Best feature: What, have you been living under a rock? It's all about the seductive bartenders dancing on the bar, obviously.

Coyote Ugly is not for people who take themselves too seriously. It is not for the uptight. It is not for the hard of hearing. It is not for the serious drinker.

So this basically leaves just a few types of bar patrons: spring breakers, tourists who should know better, and single gentlemen who do not wish to remain single for the entire evening.

We fit into a fourth group: the thirsty and morbidly curious.

Our curiosity is satisfied in less than two minutes, and our thirst is quenched in five. We order a round of beer because, well, look around: does this seem like the place for swilling cosmos?

We readily admit that Coyote Ugly is not our all-time favorite place for drinking in the Quarter. But this book isn't just about us. For you, it might be Paradise on Earth. For you, Coyote

Ugly might be just the thing to wash off the stink of a four-hour team-building seminar in Convention Hall Breakout Room G. And if it is, you're totally welcome.

Photograph by John d'Addario

Name: Crescent City Brewhouse
Address: 527 Decatur Street
Phone: 504-522-0571
Web site: www.CrescentCityBrewhouse.com
Your tab: Reasonable. Even though it's on a busy street, Crescent City Brewhouse isn't a tourist trap.
What you're swilling: The bar is well stocked, but as its name implies, it makes its own beer, with around five homegrown brews on tap at any time. The pilsner is a nice, light option for New Orleans' sultry days, and the seasonals can be downright fantastic.
What you're wearing: This is a restaurant—not a high-end joint, but a restaurant all the same. It's also pretty family friendly. There's no need to dress up, but tank tops in restaurants are always a little tacky, don't you think?
What you're hearing: Apart from the piped-in music, Crescent City often has a live jazz band playing up front. The tunes are usually from the traditional (or "trad") jazz songbook, which is perfect for dining, drinking, and conversation.
Tattoo themes: Since the place holds a mix of tourists and locals (mostly tourists), there's not really a running theme. In fact, the many moms and dads here aren't likely to display ink at all, until they reveal an ill-advised tramp stamp when bending over to pick up a diaper bag.
Your drinking buddies: Largely non-locals, but they're friendly enough. If you have a craving for a quick burger and a beer, this is one of the best places to satisfy it in this neck of the Quarter.
Best feature: The balcony on the second floor is a great spot for watching people (and the Mississippi River) go by. Drinkers are generally placed at the downstairs bar, though, so to get the prime seats, you should at least order a round of appetizers. Just be sure to time your arrival for late afternoon or evening, when the sun slips down the backside of the building.

To the casual passerby in search of an authentic New Orleans drinking experience, Crescent City Brewhouse may not look promising. It's well lit. It's family friendly. And compared to most watering holes in the Quarter, it seems disappointingly clean and new. Frankly, the Brewhouse doesn't appear all that different from chain restaurants such as Hard Rock Cafe or Bubba Gump, both of which are also located in the Vieux Carré.

But looks can be deceiving. As you walk in, you're likely to notice a jazz combo playing by the front door. It's your first clue that Crescent City Brewhouse is a genuine New Orleans product.

Your second clue is the beer selection. Like many cities, New Orleans once contained a bevy of breweries within its borders. Though most of our best-known brands have long since been laid to rest (look across the street and you'll see the former Jax Brewery, now a mall), a number of indie labels have picked up the brewmeister's torch. Abita is one, Bayou Teche is another, and Crescent City is a third.

As you can tell from the giant vats on display, Crescent City makes its beer on site—typically four house flavors plus a seasonal variety. If you're not feeling especially adventurous, go for the pilsner, which isn't all that different from most American beers. At the other end of the spectrum, there's the rich, malty "Black Forest." It's not as hearty as Guinness, but it still makes an awfully good appetizer.

Of course, there are other libations, too—a full bar, in fact. And although the menu isn't fancy in that stick-out-your-pinky, old-line New Orleans way, the food is consistently good.

Since it's late afternoon when we arrive, we ask for a table on the balcony. If we were just drinking, we'd stay down at the bar, but we're feeling peckish, so we opt for a very late dinner (or lunch, as it's called outside the South).

The sun has thankfully begun its descent, meaning that we can enjoy the view of Decatur Street and the Mississippi River beyond without having to reapply big squirts of Coppertone. Between the food and the crisp beer and the breeze, it's a perfect New Orleans moment—one that folks on the sidewalk below would never suspect.

Name: Envie
Address: 1241 Decatur Street (at Barracks Street)
Phone: 504-524-3689
Your tab: Manageable
What you're swilling: Coffee, soda, liquor, or some combination thereof
What you're wearing: Technically, this is a coffee shop, but it's also deep in the Lower French Quarter, the playground of the cool kids. You can hang out in a sweater set from Ann Taylor, but you may feel out of place.
What you're hearing: Mostly coffee-shop ambiance and the tap-tap-tap of aspiring writers hammering away on their MacBooks
Tattoo themes: Serious, varied, and impressive. These people did not just get drunk one night, wander into a studio, and pick some flash off the wall. This ink was planned.
Your drinking buddies: Locals mostly, with an abundance of younger, hipper types. Don't let that put you off, though—everyone here is pretty friendly.
Best feature: It's the anti-Starbucks. Sure, it's got coffee and pastries, but like any good European-ish café, it's got booze, too. And unlike Starbucks, people talk to you.

If you've been to Europe, you've probably been to a place like Envie. It's that curious Continental combo of bar/coffee shop that you rarely see in the U.S.

This is where we've chosen to start the night—well, the second half of it. We've just emerged from dinner half a block away, and we're heading up Decatur Street into the heart of the Quarter. We're full of gnocchi and linguine and caprese, and we're all in need of a pick-me-up. What better place to get it than at a boozy café?

The clock has just struck 10, and Envie is crowded—mostly with locals from the Quarter, the Marigny, and other nearby 'hoods. We inch up to the counter and order an array of drinks:

one shot of Maker's Mark, one café au lait, and Richard goes right up the middle, ordering an espresso with a shot of Frangelico. It's probably not great for the heart, but as the kids say: YOLO.

We toy with the idea of sitting for a minute to sip our drinks and enjoy the cool night, but every chair in the place is taken. And frankly, our duds feel dull compared to those sported by the *enfants terribles* rapt in conversation and editing their manuscripts. So, given Envie's Euro vibe, we do as we'd do across the Pond. We lean against the counter, slug our drinks, then head off into the night. (Though before leaving, we also do that most un-European of things: tip the bartender.)

Name: Felipe's

Address: 301 North Peters Street (at Bienville Street)

Phone: 504-267-4406

Website: www.FelipesTaqueria.com

Your tab: Inexpensive, until you start ordering the top-shelf tequila. And you know you will.

What you're swilling: A lot of beer—though you're welcome to mix things up. (Fun fact: Felipe's has one of the best mescal selections in the city.) If you're feeling hungry, you can step over to the adjoining restaurant and order some amazing Mexican food, which you might want to wash down with a margarita (or five).

What you're wearing: Whatever you'd wear to the mall

What you're hearing: There's usually some radio music jamming in the background, but Felipe's is at its best when there's a game on TV—a football game, a baseball game, a jai alai game (or match or rumble or whatever those things are called). The atmosphere is convivial, the bathrooms are clean, and more chips and salsa are always close at hand.

Tattoo themes: You're on Decatur Street at a de facto sports bar. Anything's possible.

Your drinking buddies: Men, women, young, old; people who've wandered in off the street to quench their thirst; some off-duty workers from the restaurant. Politicians would call it a gorgeous mosaic. We call it a great place for anonymous tippling.

Best feature: The location is hard to beat, but the stellar, super-affordable food and fantastic tequila selection are at the top of the list.

There aren't many sports bars in the French Quarter—except during Saints games, when every bar's a sports bar. Even Felipe's isn't what we'd call a real "sports bar," but whoever possesses the remote controls for the big-screen TVs clearly has a fondness for ESPN. There's always some program on the tube touting the thrill of victory and the agony of defeat.

But that's not why we like Felipe's—not really. We like Felipe's because of the adjoining restaurant, which serves up some of the best bar food in the Quarter.

When the three of us walk in, there's not much of a crowd. It's the middle of the week, and there's no big game on TV. Most of the tourists have ambled back to their hotels for post-shopping/pre-dinner naps. Which is fine—that means more room for us. We order a few beers, and Richard asks Elizabeth and Allison if they're hungry. (Like all Southerners, he's solicitous to a fault.)

"We could eat," they answer in unison.

Richard pops over to the restaurant counter and orders a few items from the menu—chips, of course, some flautas, a flan, and a very large glass of horchata. If you've ever tried to make horchata, you know it's more complicated than it seems. It requires a lot of fiddling with rice flour and cinnamon and chilling overnight. That's way too much work to put into a beverage that's not even alcoholic.

Thankfully, the resident Horchata Meister at Felipe's has the process down to a science—a thoroughly delicious science. Within 10 minutes, Richard wanders back to the counter and orders two more glasses, because Elizabeth and Allison keep slugging away at his.

In fact, the grub is so good and the environment so comfortable and unpretentious that we sit for another hour or so, moving from horchatas to margaritas when Elizabeth informs us that Felipe's has one of the best tequila selections in the Quarter. We happily sip our reposado-based drinks and nibble on some of the best flan in the city until someone finds the remote control and flips over to a bowling tournament. That's our cue. Flan be damned. You have to draw the line somewhere.

Name: Finnegan's
Address: 717 St. Peter Street
Phone: 504-599-9898
Web site: www.finneganseasy.com
Your tab: Five to six dollars per drink, including tip
What you're swilling: Half-and-halfs
What you're wearing: T-shirt
What you're hearing: Fuel, Tool, Creed on the jukebox
When you're there: Evening, night
Tattoo themes: Barbed wire, white-boy tribal
Your drinking buddies: Your buddies
Best feature: The little courtyard

A small confession: Tipplers can be snobs—not in an haute, classist, exclusive sort of way, but we can be particular about, even dismissive of, looks that don't conform to our notions of French Quarterdom. So it's not surprising that, at first, we turn a disapproving eye to Finnegan's (not be confused with Flanagan's), just half a block off Bourbon. Finnegan's is a self-proclaimed Irish bar. However, aside from the Guinness and Harp on tap, it's hard to associate the Emerald Isle with Finnegan's peach-colored walls, questionable '80s pendant lighting, white tiles, and tired jukebox. It's so hard, in fact, that we can't remember the Irish name of this bar for three days after our visit.

But even more, it's hard to connect this clean, well-lighted place to the French Quarter. Though many reviewers refer to Finnegan's as a *dive*, it's far too scrubbed and bright for that. Nor does it have the other qualities we associate with the Quarter—bohemian or chic or clever or upscale or antiquated. And for the record, the Web site's photograph is misleadingly *tawny* in its coloring. So at first, the Tipplers are tempted to exclude Finnegan's from our pages; it feels like a bar that belongs someplace else, as though they haven't tried to respect the spirit of the Quarter. Looking at its Web-site caption, "South Beach Comes to New Orleans," we learn that Finnegan's is indeed part of a small chain, with three bars in Miami. The peach walls begin to make sense.

But perhaps our nostril flaring is rooted a bit deeper, a slightly nasty thing that emerges once you've lived in New Orleans for a few years. It has to do with the staunch dividing line between the Big Easy and its more conservative suburbs. Finnegan's may have high ceilings and the long, narrow footprint of a historic building, but its *newish* look is *suburban,* and that's enough to evoke the longstanding division between the Crescent City and its environs. From their side, suburbanites peer over and see crime, trash, and ghettos; from our side, we see white flight, good old boys, and gun shows. Of course, similar lines exist between big cities and smaller towns all over America.

Naturally both views are exaggerations, but that doesn't change the fact that there are genuine differences. In this context, we Tipplers are too quick to size up and fall back on suburban profiling—noting the lack of a diverse crowd, the thick cigarette smoke, a camo top, the cupped bills of baseball caps. Despite our desire to think of ourselves as open-minded, perhaps one of the qualities that makes us feel "at home" at a bar is our very similarity, real or perceived, to those around us.

But at some point during our second round, Finnegan's makes a comeback, because we haven't left, and (perhaps this is the *Irish* part) we're still drinking. We're forced to nibble on some humble pie as we admit that we haven't vacated our stools for any of the other open shutters along St. Peter Street that would require, say, 10 steps to reach. Finnegan's is located on a block so packed with bars that you could become quite stricken by simply indulging in a single round at every one located within 100 feet of its doors.

But we don't leave. So perhaps *a clean, well-lighted place* isn't such a bad thing after all. And maybe sometimes a bar isn't anything but a bar. There's been a steady flow of patrons in and out, and the energy at Finnegan's remains upbeat. We consider other plusses, not the least of which are cheap drinks, all under five dollars. And then there's a small menu of the kinds of brown fried things a Tippler might want to crunch on come midnight and just as reasonably priced as our half-and-halfs. And though we feel certain that most of the drinkers aren't locals, for the record, we've heard that a few of the Quarter's musicians and service-industry folk do make their way into Finnegan's for a little release.

Best of all, we're glad we stayed long enough to seek out the facilities, which, like much pre-indoor-plumbing architecture, require a trip out back. It's then that we discover that Finnegan's does have a genuine connection to the French Quarter—a small courtyard. The Tipplers decide to tipple here, positioning ourselves away from the bad ocean-themed mural and instead facing the brick walls, a leafy tree, and the overhead servant's gallery. For a few minutes, Finnegan's feels quintessentially Vieux Carré—a quaint, shaded refuge from the crowds of nearby Bourbon and the perfect spot for a little snobbery.

Name: MRB and Grill
Address: 515 St. Philip Street
Phone: 504-524-2558
Your tab: Cheap
What you're swilling: MRB is a neighborhood bar, with a splash of sports bar dabbed behind its ears. In a place like this, you can't go wrong with beer—but hey, don't let us tell you what to drink.
What you're wearing: Come as you are, but be prepared for a fairly aggressive air-conditioning system. If you're the sort of person who tends to complain about being cold, bring a shawl or sweatshirt.
What you're hearing: More likely than not, whatever game is on television
Tattoo themes: On the one hand, you're in the French Quarter, where tattoos are *de rigueur*. On the other hand, no one at MRB really cares.
Your drinking buddies: Mostly locals, with the occasional group of tourists trundling up to the bar for a round of hurricanes. Don't worry: they leave quickly.
Best feature: First, there's the food, which is nearly as good as Coop's around the corner. (Try the étouffée—seriously.) Second, MRB has an unofficial mascot: an awesome, three-legged dog. Together, the two may not be entirely legal, but we won't tell if you don't.

MRB sits in a gray area between the loud, boisterous Upper Quarter (centered around Bourbon Street) and the equally loud but far more local Lower Quarter (centered around Decatur Street). That makes it the perfect midpoint to stop in and freshen up your drink when you're traveling from one zone to the other. This is, in fact, why we're here—that and the fact that Richard really needs a bathroom, and given its out-of-the-way location, MRB isn't usually crowded.

While he scampers off to do his thing, Elizabeth and Allison ditch the dregs of their daiquiris and order a round of beer from MRB's impressive selection. The dude next to them tries to strike up a conversation.

"So, are you from around here?" Apparently guys still use this line.

"Yes, we are," chirps Elizabeth. "I live in the Bywater, and Allison lives Uptown." From her expression, it's impossible to know if she's flirting or toying with the poor schmuck.

"I don't know where that is. I'm from Ohio," he says.

"Oh, a swinger's state!" puns Elizabeth. She's definitely toying.

The young man looks confused, then the clouds pass. "Oh, like in elections and stuff. I thought you meant something else." He smirks shyly. "You know . . . like swinging." He's making this far too easy.

Just then Richard returns, wrapped in a silk bathrobe and followed by a three-legged dog. "Can you believe someone would just abandon this in a bathroom stall?" he asks, rubbing the robe's well-worn lapels.

"Yes, but we can't believe you'd put it on without at least running it through the rinse cycle," says Allison.

Richard scowls, then points to Mr. Ohio as though he weren't two feet away. "Who's your friend?"

"I'm Steve," the guy responds. "Who's that?" he asks, pointing at the pooch.

"I don't know, Daddy. He followed me home. Can I keep him?" Richard grins, thinking he's being cute, but Ohio shakes his head and wanders off.

Mr. Ohio, if you're reading this, please come back. Things were just getting interesting.

Photograph by John d'Addario

Name: Pirate's Alley Café

Address: 622 Pirate's Alley

Phone: 504-524-9332

Web site: www.piratesalleycafe.com

Your tab: Five dollars per drink, reasonable for this part of the Quarter

What you're swilling: A mixed drink

What you're wearing: Whatever you're wearing

What you're hearing: "Arrr!"

When you're there: Afternoon or evening, following your guided tour

Tattoo themes: Skulls and crossbones

Your drinking buddies: Swashbucklers

Best feature: Location, location, location, and, of course, pirates

It's a dark and stormy night. Really, it is a dark and stormy night, typical of New Orleans in July, the monsoon season. On nights like these, the Quarter takes on a different persona—darker, edgier, moody as a Parisian, but, of course, hot as ever. As we walk through the streets towards Pirate's Alley, lightning cracks the sky. Thunder breaks and the downpour begins, the rain so thick it appears to shroud the buildings. The sewers and drainpipes begin to roil.

For a moment, there is confusion, especially among the tourists. A young woman desperately asks where we got our umbrella. A haunted-history tour huddles together, the participants slowly sweating to death in their plastic ponchos. This is not the vision of New Orleans the postcards promise—the one of aimlessly wandering the colorful sunny streets with a hurricane in hand. No, these are the warm-ups, the reminders that hurricanes are more than colorful drinks; they are real.

But on this evening, the rickshaw drivers pedal furiously towards shelter, while a veteran tarot-card reader calmly pulls her small table into the lee of a balcony. Over the small flame of her candle, she stares down the dark street. Presumably she saw it all coming.

Seeking shelter from the storm, the battered crew enters the tavern. Okay, perhaps not battered, but shoes are wet and hair is definitely afrizz. Others follow us inside. The regular bartender, an attentive, pretty blonde who somehow manages to make her scarlet stomacher and headscarf look tasteful, keeps the arched doors open—all four sets of them—and we can see the rain bouncing on the pavers just a few feet away. For the record, the Web-site photos are heavy on pirates and don't do the architecture justice.

If it wasn't raining and still afternoon, we'd likely see patrons sitting at the tables outside, and they would appear content to do absolutely nothing but take in the quaintness of this heart-wrenchingly charming spot in the Quarter. And this evening, if we could look past the requisite net, ship's wheel, and peg-legged, eye-patched, salty-dog statue on the bar top, we might imagine we were in some picturesque corner *tabac* in old Montmartre. The Pirate's Alley Café is delightfully petite, a twin-sized bed of a bar that can seat about eight at the counter and maybe four more at a couple of bistro tables inside. Not surprisingly, this is also the end spot for most of the dark-arts tours, whether they be haunted, vampiric, or piratical.

At times, we catch a faint mist on our backs. Summer rains like these make a Tippler grateful for the simple comforts of a stool, a drink, and decent conversation to wait out the storm. A heavily tattooed and bald and, yes, faintly piratey lad two stools down sits with the ease of a regular. In the five minutes of our knowing him, he's told us the location of the two swinger bars in the Central Business District and that we wouldn't *believe* the things he has seen.

Yo ho ho and a bottle of rum. A young trio seeking shelter inquires about shots from the bottle marked *Toxic Baby*. The label shows a skull and crossbones. The bartender sets a plastic baby (like the ones hidden in Mardi Gras king cakes) on the rim of each glass and pours out a dark-brown, viscous liquid.

"What's it made out of?" it finally occurs to them to ask.

The bartender turns the bottle and points to the back label, and we all lean in: *Made from the most cost-effective ingredients known.*

The Tipplers choose to stay away from Toxic Baby. Instead, we sip whiskeys and stare at a favorite Quarter view—across the narrow alley at a backlit St. Louis Cathedral, bright and white against the dark sky. It's a visible reminder that New Orleans is a city of proximate extremes—wealth and poverty, life and death, the sacred and the profane. Elsewhere it might be unusual for a bar and a church to nestle so closely, but not here. In New Orleans, both have claims to prime turf.

Name: Port of Call
Address: 838 Esplanade Avenue (at Dauphine Street)
Phone: 504-523-0120
Web site: www.PortOfCallNOLA.com
Your tab: Fair to middling
What you're swilling: They have a full bar, but many of your drinking buddies will be slugging monsoons—Port of Call's answer to Pat O'Brien's hurricane. At $10, they're not cheap, but you don't need many to get completely lit. And you get to keep the souvenir plastic go-cup. So, you know, that's something.
What you're wearing: Casual togs
What you're hearing: More than anything, you're likely to hear the crowd chatting away. Despite the decor, we've never heard patrons break out into a sea shanty.
Tattoo themes: It's hard to say. The low lighting is great for drinking but not so much for spotting ink trends.
Your drinking buddies: Mostly local, with a heavy emphasis on 20-somethings, who've often just come from some sporting event or other
Best feature: We love a good nautical/pirate-decor theme, don't you?

If you're looking to party, this may not be the place for you. The drinks are good, and yes, the patrons are friendly. But thanks to Port of Call's legendary hamburgers, it can get awfully crowded, especially around mealtimes. That goes double on weekends.

Thankfully, that's not when we're visiting. It's a beautiful Thursday in the middle of March, and we've decided to play hooky. At 2:00 in the afternoon, this end of the Quarter is fairly quiet, the birds are chirping, and the sweet olive is in bloom. Naturally, we decide to head indoors.

Richard is always amused by Port of Call's decor, accented with ropes and netting and the kind of shaded lanterns more commonly seen at fish camps along the Gulf Coast, or maybe in quaint restaurants on Cape Cod. Without thinking, he breaks into the chorus of a long-forgotten John Denver tune—"Aye, *Calypso,* I sing to your spirit, the men who have served you so long and so well"—then trails off because Allison and Elizabeth look at him as if he's already drunk. (Note: he is not, yet.)

Since we've got a long day of goofing off ahead of us, we consider a nice, refreshing round of beers, but seeing other patrons with their white-plastic go-cups reminds us of Port of Call's other claim to fame: Neptune's monsoon. It isn't a particularly elegant drink. It's a lot like a hurricane, which used to be fairly fancy-schmancy, but is now made with well-brand clear liquors and a heaping helping of low-rent fruit punch. The hurricane, however, has the saving grace of being served in a charming glass. The monsoon, not so much. But we don't really care. The walk over has made us thirsty, and the monsoon is just what we need—well, that and maybe a burger or two.

Name: Red Fish Grill
Address: 115 Bourbon Street
Phone: 504-598-1200
Web site: www.RedFishGrill.com
Your tab: Compared to some of the other joints on Bourbon Street, this place is a bargain.
What you're swilling: Whatever you like—Red Fish has a very, very full bar.
What you're wearing: There's no dress code to speak of, but Red Fish is far more low-key than the bars you'll find a few blocks down Bourbon. Dress as though you're going to a restaurant, which is what Red Fish is.
What you're hearing: Between all the right angles and the concrete floors, it's noisy in here, even when the crowd is sparse.
Tattoo themes: During the lunch hour, there's no theme to speak of, but at night, Red Fish seems to get a little more "collegiate," so, you know, whatever frat boys have inked on their biceps.
Your drinking buddies: Like Bourbon House across the way, Red Fish draws a mix of locals and tourists for lunch. By sundown, though, it's mostly youngish out-of-towners.
Best feature: The food is great. Sure, once you get a little tipsy, you might be tempted to hit up the Krystal burger joint across the street, but stay put. There's a reason the Brennan family has so many restaurants.

Let's be honest: the first block of Bourbon Street isn't much to look at. Unlike other stretches of the strip, the offerings here are pretty slim. In fact, most people zoom through pretty quickly without noticing much beyond the Krystal burger joint.

Thankfully, we know better. We've just come from an event in the Central Business District on the other side of Canal Street and are en route to a party at the far end of the Quarter. Just for kicks, we've opted to take Bourbon instead of our usual Royal Street path, but to survive the throngs, we need to steel our nerves.

A quick detour into Red Fish Grill does the trick. Ordinarily, the smell of tequila turns Richard's stomach, but considering where we are, downing a shot of the stuff seems obligatory. Just to be safe, we each do two. Before our buzzes start to wane, we pour our beer chasers into go-cups and head back out into the crowd, weaving our way down Bourbon—literally.

Name: Sidney's Wine Cellar
Address: 917 Decatur Street
Phone: 504-524-6872
Your tab: Moderate, though the beer prices are some of the best in the Quarter.
What you're swilling: Beer, wine, and spirits—they sell it all. Get your beer to go.
What you're wearing: Whatever you are willing to go grocery shopping in
What you're hearing: Beer recommendations
Tattoo themes: They run the gamut.
Your drinking buddies: Fellow shoppers, both tourists and locals
Best feature: Wide beer selection

New Orleans doesn't just offer 24-hour ready access to booze—you can take your drink with you wherever you go. Locals often grab a "walking-around drink" to savor while chatting with neighbors, walking the dog, or heading home from a favorite neighborhood watering hole. Drinking while walking allows you to fully appreciate all that's lovely around you: beautiful architecture, swinging music, or someone in a pirate costume on a random Thursday.

Most go-cups are found in the French Quarter, and one of our favorite places to pick up a to-go drink is Sidney's. Located under the mighty protection of the golden statue of Joan of Arc, Sidney's offers one of the best (and best-priced) single-beer selections in the city.

The Tipplers pop into Sidney's one Saturday afternoon, unsure of where we are headed but certain it involves a beer along the way. From the outside, Sidney's resembles the myriad of corner stores that pepper the Quarter, but its prodigious beer selection sets it apart from its more commonplace competitors. Sidney's stock includes the typical American brewing giants, but their coolers also house beers from around the globe: Chimay,

Spaten Optimator, and Paulaner Salvator fill the shelves. Today we dip into their wide selection of local beers, and our total bill is $6.30, including our plastic go-cups.

If beer isn't your thing, or if you are stocking up for a party in your hotel room, Sidney's also sells spirits and features a shelf with everything you need to make some iconic New Orleans cocktails, including Sazerac rye, Herbsaint, Peychaud's Bitters, and Pimm's.

We conclude our purchase and head towards the river to enjoy the first cool breeze of fall and some good music from the street musicians who play on the levee. Before we even cross Decatur, our gait slows and we brake to inspect the artwork on the Jackson Square fence and pet a buggy mule. These pauses punctuate the rest of our stroll on a lovely autumnal day, made better with beer.

Name: Vieux Carré Wine & Spirits
Address: 422 Chartres Street
Phone: 504-568-9463
Your tab: Varies
What you're swilling: On site? Probably beer. Back at the hotel? Anything you want. (See below.)
What you're wearing: They're not here to judge. They're here to sell you booze.
What you're hearing: The chatter of the proprietors as they offer suggestions on reds, whites, sparkling wines, and harder stuff. There might be a little radio music in the background, but dancing is neither appropriate nor encouraged.
Tattoo themes: None
Your drinking buddies: Service-industry workers who've just finished a shift at one of the nearby bars, restaurants, or hotels and need to take the edge off
Best feature: Best liquor selection in the Quarter, bar none

Vieux Carré Wine & Spirits isn't technically a bar. It's a liquor store, with a great selection of spirits—anything you might need for a night of partying. If you're looking to host a get-together in your hotel room before heading out for a night on the town, this is the place to stock up.

But Vieux Carré also has a selection of beer and wine in a cooler at the front of the store. And conveniently, they have a small table with a couple of chairs where you can sit for a spell and suck down your purchase. Drinking here feels a little like going to wine shops in Italy, where the *antipasti* keep coming, so long as you keep drinking. Alas, there's no food here, but the proprietors' Italian accents contribute to the vibe. If you need a quick pick-me-up and don't mind downing your beverage of choice under fluorescent lights, this is the place to go.

CHAPTER 11

Tippler Favorites

We're often asked for a short list of our favorite bars. This is a difficult, even painful task. Such a list leaves out many places that we frequent and would never want to be without. After all, *limiting* ourselves is counterintuitive to the indulgent spirit of the French Quarter.

That said, the following bars are exceptionally dear to our hearts and livers. These places draw us, for better or worse, again and again. Some are fancy and some are not, and we advise reading the entries before trying them. However, these bars all share a distinct character that feels inextricably linked to the French Quarter.

The Dungeon
Erin Rose
Fahy's
French 75
Fritzel's European Jazz Pub
    (Maison Bourbon is a close second)
Good Friends Bar
Krazy Korner
Napoleon House
One Eyed Jacks
Pirate's Alley Café
Sazerac Bar
Sylvain

Index